JOSIAH WARREN – THE FIRST AMERICAN ANARCHIST
"THE REMARKABLE AMERICAN"

Magdalena Modrzejewska

JOSIAH WARREN –
THE FIRST AMERICAN ANARCHIST

"THE REMARKABLE AMERICAN"

Kraków

Reviewer:
dr hab. Paweł Laidler

Cover design:
Paweł Sepielak

Picture of Josiah Warren used on the cover comes from
the Labadie Collection, University of Michigan

ISBN 978-83-7638-808-3

Publikacja finansowana ze środków grantu Narodowego Centrum Nauki
na projekt "Josiah Warren - pierwszy amerykański anarchista?"
(UMO-2011/01/D/HS5/01660)

KSIĘGARNIA AKADEMICKA
ul. św. Anny 6, 31-008 Kraków
tel./faks: 12 431 27 43, 12 421 13 87
e-mail: akademicka@akademicka.pl

Online bookstore:
www.akademicka.pl

TABLE OF CONTENTS

Acknowledgments

This publication and the entire research project has been made possible by the generous support of the National Science Centre from Poland. The Grant No: UMO-2011/01/D/HS5/01660. I would like to express my gratitude to the entire National Science Centre as well as the selection committee for their kind support of my research.
Some of the research hypotheses fully developed in the first chapter have been formulated in my earlier book published in Polish in 2012 (*Josiah Warren – pierwszy amerykański anarchista?*, Kraków: Wydawnictwo Uniwersytetu Jagiellońskiego).

*To the memory
of Agnes Inglis,
James Joseph Martin,
and Charles Shively*

PREFACE

Growing up in a communist country, in the city of Lodz, with its long lasting tradition of labour movement and organized strikes, one of the greatest of which ended in the revolution of 1905, I was long familiar with the anarcho-communist tradition. In the United States, I discovered a rich body of sources on the topic, sources that revealed the existence of political and philosophical tradition that focused on limiting the governmental power in order to protect individual rights of person and rights of private property even to the extent of elimination of government. I found this version of anarchism extremely intriguing as it relied entirely on the power of words and not on the power of bombs. This peaceful, philosophic movement continues to impact, directly or indirectly, American political theory and practice. Looking at the Josiah Warren I was mesmerized by the complexity and richness of his thought, as well as the boldness with which he framed and communicated his ideas. I was also impressed by the fact that he was aware of the danger of being categorized and ascribed to one philosophical movement, and did everything what was in his power to avoid that and stay truthful to his convictions.

I could not avoid looking at Warren from a European perspective, seeing him on the one hand as a *remarkable American*, on the other hand experiencing moments of astonishment that one could promote such radical individualism that left no place for any authority. The most remarkable to me was the fact that Warren formed this views on his own, independently from any other philosophic writers. For him, as for many other Americans, certain truths were self-evident.

The research project was founded by the National Science Centre but I would like to express my gratitude to many other places and institutions that offered me help and assistance. I am extremely thankful to Julie Herrada, curator of Labadie Collection at the University of Michigan; professor Casey Harrison, the director of the Center for Communal Studies, Evansville, IN; Amanda Bryden, State Historic Sites Collections Manager from the New Harmony State Historic Site for her interest in my research and her commitment to the popularization of New Harmony history, and Steve Cochran, the former head of the Working Men's Institute in New Harmony. And I especially thank the participants of the Socialism and Capitalism conference for their insightful comments on my paper. Many colleagues and friends have been of great help; I wish to recall here the useful

linguistic suggestions given by Tatyana Bakhmetyeva, Agnieszka Stasiewicz-
-Bienkowska and Tomasz Soroka.

   Warren's writings are dispersed among many places; some of them available
only on microfilm and barely legible; many of them I transcribed for the first
time. For that reason, the book offers more extensive citation than usual, in hope
of making Warren's writing more accessible to other scholars working on this
subject.

INTRODUCTION –
OR WHO IS JOSIAH WARREN?

> „I can compare Mr. Warren with no other man I have
> met. Simple as a child, wise as the Gods. He reverses
> Socrates method. Instead of asking, he answers questions.
> Old Socrates himself I think would retreat from such
> a contest, and spending some time with his Xantippe,
> confess that for once he had been completely floored.
> And yet, he would have to return, for Mr. Warren makes
> no enemies."

Sidney H. Morse, Word vol. 2, no. 1, May 1873.

Who was Josiah Warren? It is unfortunate that such a question needs to be asked, and such an important political thinker as Warren had been overlooked and nearly forgotten.[1] But there is another reason to ask this question. Who was Josiah Warren? How can one describe him or put in a particular category? Was he a dogmatic political thinker or a revolutionary practitioner? Was he the first American anarchist, or perhaps a forerunner of libertarianism? Would it be more accurate to associate him with socialism or egalitarian liberalism? Was he a brilliant social reformer, or just a fanatic zealot? Was he a genius or simply insane? This confusion seems common for scholars, regretfully very few of them; study Josiah Warren. For those who attempted to describe him in the nineteenth century Warren was the first American anarchist. That is how he was identified by his disciple, Stephen Pearl Andrews,[2] and later by Benjamin Ricketson Tucker,[3] the

---

[1] K.T. Fann writing about Alexander Bryan Johnson expressed the same outrage about the fact that such a prominent figure as Johnson has been forgotten. It is surprising that so many prominent American nineteenth century intellectuals, widely known and appreciated in the United States and famous abroad have been so heavily neglected over time. See. K.T. Fann, "Alexander Bryan Johnson (1786-1867): The First Linguistic Philosopher," *The Semiotic Web 1989*, ed. Thomas A. Sebeok, and Jean Umiker-Sebeok (Berlin, New York: De Gruyter, 1990) 31.

[2] Stephen Pearl Andrews, unpublished manuscript entitled *Sociology*, box 1. Andrews papers, Andrews Papers, State Historical Society of Wisconsin, Madison, Wisconsin, undated, archival material.

[3] Benjamin R. Tucker, "On Picked Duty," *Liberty, not the Daughter but the Mother of Order*, 14.3 (Dec. 1900): 1.

label that was firmly ascribed to him after the publication in 1906 of his first biography *Josiah Warren- First American Anarchist* by William Bailie.

Some scholars, such as Eunice Schuster,[4] William O. Reichert[5] and David De Leon[6] placed Warren within the American individualist anarchist tradition. Others, such as Nathan Jun or Crispin Sartwell observed with some discontent that Warren and his movement had "been co-opted by right-wing libertarian ideologues".[7] Many scholars and journalists put Warren within the libertarian anti--statist theory, just between Tucker and Nozick.[8] But these attempts to categorize Warren and squeeze him into a certain narrow frame mostly failed. One reason for this persistent difficulty was because Warren himself despised all labels and all *–isms*; "we want no more isms," he wrote in 1854.[9] More importantly it was because Warren's thought is so rich that it evades categorization, and all attempts of labelling this philosophy result in oversimplifications of its richness. Warren is neither left nor right. There are elements of his philosophy that are leftist, like drive to equitability. There are also elements of his thought that are rightist like his uncompromising commitment to the right of liberty and property.

Perhaps one of the best description is offered by John Stuart Mill who describes Warren simply as "a remarkable American".[10] This statement perfectly summarizes both Warren's uniqueness and the fact that his life and his ideas were so deeply

---

[4] Eunice Schuster, *Native American Anarchism: A Study of Left-Wing American Individualism*, Smith College Studies in History (Northampton, Mass.: Department of History of Smith College, 1931-1932) v. 17, no. 1-4.

[5] William O. Reichert, *Partisans of Freedom: A Study in American Anarchism* (Bowling Green, Ohio: Bowling Green University Popular Press, 1976).

[6] David DeLeon, *The American As Anarchist: Reflections on Indigenous Radicalism* (Baltimore: Md. Johns Hopkins University, 1978).

[7] Nathan Jun, rev. of *The Practical Anarchist: Writing of Josiah Warren*, by Crispin Sartwell, *Anarchist Studies* 20:1, Spring-Summer 2012: 115. When contemporary scholars use the term libertarianism to analyze Native American tradition (applying the term coined by Eunice Schuster) they quite often use this term anachronistically. But in the nineteenth century and even in early twentieth century libertarian was defined just as the "one who upholds the principle of liberty, especially individual liberty of thought and action", as the Charles Sprading argued in the 1913. If we apply such definition, then undoubtedly Warren can be called libertarian. Cf. Charles T. Sprading, *Liberty and the Great Libertarians. An Anthology on Liberty, a Handbook of Freedom* (Los Angeles: published for the author) 5.

[8] Robert Nozick was familiar with Josiah Warren's work, and mentioned him once in the part dedicated to utopia in his *Anarchy, State and Utopia*. He also referred to Spooner and Tucker writings that "discusse operation of a social system in which all protective functions are privately supplied". In the same passage Nozick admits that "It cannot be overemphasized how lively, stimulating, and interesting are the writings and arguments of Spooner and Tucker". So there is no doubt about the influence of Tucker and Spooner on Warren. Cf. Robert Nozick, *Anarchy, State, and Utopia* (New York: Basic Books, 1974) 316, 335-336. Tucker dedicated his book to the Josiah Warren, therefore we can trace the existing parallel.

[9] Josiah Warren, "To Enquirers." *Periodical Letter*, 1:2 (Aug. 1854): 20.

[10] Charles Shively, used this phrase as a title of his BA thesis pertinent to Josiah Warren but John Stuart Mill coined this label for Josiah Warren, cf. John Stuart Mill, *Collected Works of John Stuart Mill*, Vol. 1: *Autobiography and Literary Essay*, edited by John M. Robson and Jack Stillinger (Toronto: University of Toronto Press) 260.

embedded in American tradition of political thought and political practice. When John Stuart Mill mentioned Josiah Warren in his Autobiography, he depicted him as the person who "had framed a System of Society, on the foundation of 'the Sovereignty of the individual'(…) bearing a superficial resemblance to some of the projects of Socialists", but "is diametrically opposite to them in principle, since it recognizes no authority whatever in Society over the individual, except to enforce equal Freedom of development for all individualities".[11] Mill admitted that he borrowed from the Warrenites their phrase, the sovereignty of the individual.[12]

In his work, Warren raised eternal questions: how to define human nature, what is the purpose of human life, who is the sovereign, what are the limits of power, what are the limits of liberty, can we reconcile equality and liberty, what is the appropriate and just reward for labour. And to these eternal questions he offers creative, radical, uncompromising answers. Warren's genius manifests itself also in the fact that he anticipated many later ideas. His theory refined its shape in 1827-28: he appraised individualism almost a decade before Emerson; he practiced mutualism almost a decade before Proudhon fully developed his theory; he demanded equality for women more than a decade before Seneca Fall, and he consequently used the gender equal term "he/she" more than century before political correctness made it common.

According to William Reichert, "Warren [was] struggling with the difficult problem of reconciling liberty and equality in such a way that neither would be compromised".[13] He found a way to do it, not only theoretically, but also practically through his socio-economic experiments. Rooting his theory from the appraisal of individuals and differences among them he found the way of keeping liberty that is not coerced by any external factors. What drives dramatically distinct individuals to cooperate peacefully is their pursuit of happiness. Such happiness, Warren thought, can be obtain only in cooperation with others, through mutual assistance, not in solitude.

Warren believed that individuals were naturally inclined to cooperation. Therefore, his system provided conditions where individual liberties would not be violated and there would be no need for any external coercion. Voluntarism was the only acceptable form of social relations. Norms were recognized individually, based on the principle of individual sovereignty and responsibility, where human beings make decisions and bear all responsibility for their actions. Sovereignty in Warren's theory is non-transferrable, a logical consequence of his demand for personal responsibility for actions we take.

In their pursuit of happiness individuals are not unrestrained selfish agents. They reject taking advantage of their privileged positions, because in the future it can deprive them of the assistance of others in pursuit of their happiness. Inspired

---

[11] Mill, *Autobiography* 260.
[12] Mill, *Autobiography* 261.
[13] Reichert, *Partisans* 66.

by Adam Smith's theory that labour determines the price, Warren went further, suggesting the system of labour for labour exchange. Using Judeo-Christian tradition that perceived income based on speculation not on work as immoral, Warren also made cost of the production limit of price.

Warren was an exceptional person, a visionary, a dreamer, a prophet. A highly charismatic figure, he was at the same time faithful to his individualistic principles, and he refused to impose his opinions on others. He creatively sought for innovative social, political, economic or technological solutions, which helped to execute ideals of liberty and equity with pursuit of happiness and self--development. Familiar with the European intellectual tradition, Warren seemed to be more attracted to the American one, and in his philosophy exhibited Puritan and Jeffersonian elements. Therefore, work was essential and sole title to profit, as well as self-restrain and modesty were highly appraised as desirable virtues. At the same time those ideals would be reconcilable with the demand for individual happiness and self-excellence.[14]

Was he a heartless father and husband who repeatedly abandoned his family for a couple of years? Was he a severe father who refused his children breakfast if they did not work for it? Was he a recluse and a radical individualist who never let his relationships, including his family relationships, verify the claim that an individual and his/her needs, which included himself and his needs, were the most important ones? His entire life was an incessant testing of his theories. He lived as he preached, and even though he did not impose his vision on others, he was uncompromising in his quest for it. Thanks to his personal charm, he was surrounded by a group of followers and disciples. "Simple as a child, wise as the Gods", "a remarkable American" – this might be the most accurate portrait of Josiah Warren.

---

[14] Donald E. Frey, "Individualist Economic Values and Self-Interest: the Problem in the Puritan Ethic," *Journal of Business Ethics* 17 (1998): 1573–1580.

TURBULENT TIMES –
TOWARD INTELLECTUAL TURMOIL[15]

In the early 1800s, a young American republic faced unprecedented conflicts and changes in the sphere of economics and social organisation, conflicts and changes that demanded intellectual redefinition of how to organise political, social and economic order. In that context, Warren's radicalism appears as part of a comprehensive and nationwide attempt to redefine republican ideals and adjust them to contemporaneous situations and challenges. Warren's solution to social problems emerges as one of many voices in the discussion about how to define concepts essential to the functioning of capitalism like labour, cost, value, competition or cooperation.

One of the most noticeable phenomena of the early 1800s was the rapid industrialisation. Data shows that in less than a decade the number of business incorporations doubled or tripled. As Clyman A. Haulman reports, "business incorporations in the states of New York, New Jersey, Pennsylvania and Maryland, which had averaged twenty-six per year for the period 1800–6, jumped to fifty--four new firms per year in 1807–11 with a peak of eighty-three in 1811".[16] In the same time frame, the production of certain goods rose over 900%; for example, the "[c]otton spindles which stood at 8,000 in 1807 rose to 87,000 by 1810 and to 130,000 in 1815, while the number of bales of cotton used in factories rose from an estimated 10,000 in 1810 to 90,000 in 1815".[17] This increase resulted in remarkable changes of the market itself and of the economic exchange.

Recent historical research suggests a shift in the categories of open conflict between the pro- and anti-market advocates.[18] Starting with the path-breaking

---

[15] I decided to add this part after reading Charles Shively's unpublished thesis, *A Remarkable American: Josiah Warren, 1798-1874* from the 1959. His writings persuaded me to put more emphasis on early American economy and the time of the early 1800s. The current state of research also allows to look at Warren's experiments as part of broader attempts to define and redefine the core elements of capitalism as labour, cost, value, competition and cooperation. Cf. Charles Shively "A Remarkable American: Josiah Warren 1798-1874", diss. Harvard University, 1959.

[16] Clyde A. Haulman, *Virginia and the Panic of 1819: The First Great Depression and the Commonwealth* (London: Pickering & Chatto, 2008) 8.

[17] Haulman 8.

[18] The excellent summary of the historians' discussion and perspectives on this development is provided by Appleby, see: Joyce Appleby, "The Vexed Story of Capitalism Told by American

Charles Beard's *An Economic Interpretation of the Constitution of the United States*,[19] the first work, according to Joyce Oldham Appleby, that identified the juxtaposition and "thus separated the economy of commercial agriculture—the capitalism of the many—from the investments of bankers and merchants—the capitalism of the few—choreographing capitalism's entrance into American history through the fancy footwork of an elite attentive to its vested interests".[20] It is not that the market did not exist before this turbulent time, but the events of the early 1800s became formative in the creation of the capitalist market as we know it today. As John Lauritz Larson pointed out, "Before the market revolution, there were markets, to be sure: Profits were taken, greed exhibited, goods produced and exchanged. But greed was not normative, and an individual's behavior might as often contradict as conform to the dictates of economic interest".[21]

The market activities in the early 1800s were rarely put into the frame of and bound by the notions of virtue, self-perfection and moderation. In the last few decades there has been a growing interest in this phenomenon of economy of Early Republic, and a substantial body of literature has been developed since the 1960s revealing a more complex nature as well as the compound character of the entrepreneurial activities of the period. These almost "revisionist" works showed that perceiving the economy of the early American Republic through the cliché of contemporary perception of capitalism is both oversimplified and anachronistic.

It led to creating a new research approach, that was called "new social history", putting emphasis on the explanatory role that political economy started to play coalesced with history. The most comprehensive exposition of such research is presented in James L. Huston's *Economic Landscapes Yet to be Discovered: The*

Historians," *Journal of the Early Republic.*21 (2001) 1-18. The discussion about the notion of the market as well as the quest for co-relations between republicanism and liberalism is at Appleby's other pieces: Joyce Appleby, "Liberalism and the American Revolution," *New England Quarterly* (Mar. 1976): 3-26; Joyce Appleby, "The Social Origins of American Revolutionary Ideology," *Journal of American History* 64 (Mar. 1978): 935-958; Joyce Appleby, *Capitalism and a New Social Order: The Republican Vision of the 1790s.* (New York: New York University Press, 1984); Charles Sellers, *The Market Revolution: Jacksonian America, 1815-1846* (New York: Oxford University Press, 1991); James Henretta, "The 'Market' in the Early Republic," *Journal of the Early Republic* 18.2 (1998): 289--304; Sean Wilentz, "Society, Politics and the Market Revolution, 1815-1848," *The New American History*, ed. Eric Foner (Philadelphia: Temple University Press, 1991) 61-84; Sean Wilentz, *Major Problems in the Early Republic: 1787-1848; Documents and Essays* (Boston: Houghton Mifflin, 2008); Paul E. Johnson, "The Market Revolution," *Encyclopedia of American Social History 3 Volumes*, vol. 1. eds. Mary K. Cayton, Elliot J. Gorn, Peter W. Williams (New York: Scribner, 1993) 545-560; Michael Merrill, "The Anticapitalist Origins of the United States," *Review Fernand Braudel Center* 13.4 (1990): 465-497; Henry Watson, "The Market and Its Discontents," *Journal of the Early Republic* 12.4 (1992): 464-470.

[19]   Charles A. Beard, *An Economic Interpretation of the Constitution of the United States* (New York: Macmillan Co., 1913).

[20]   Appleby, *The Vexed* 2.

[21]   John L. Larson, *The Market Revolution in America: Liberty, Ambition, and the Eclipse of the Common Good* (Cambridge: Cambridge University Press, 2010) 9.

Early American Republic and Historians' Unsubtle Adoption of Political Economy.[22] It is also worth mentioning Paul Gilje's *Rise of Capitalism in the Early Republic.* As Gilje said, "In surveying the rise of capitalism in the early republic, we must be aware that in this period capitalism itself remained in its adolescence. Vibrant, cocky, feeling its own strength, and ready to take on the world, it was not the full-blown mature system of billion-dollar corporations, industrial development, urban sprawl, and intricate international financing that took shape by the end of the century. Yet as we stare into the exuberance of its youth, we can delineate many of the outlines of the capitalist system far more clearly than we could from its embryonic earlier expressions in the colonial and medieval periods. (...). More than that, it was in this period that many of the later elements of capitalism (...) began to take on a recognizable shape".[23] These works showed that the Early

---

[22] James L. Huston, "Economic Landscapes yet to Be Discovered: the Early American Republic and Historians' Unsubtle Adoption of Political Economy," *Journal of the Early Republic* 24.2 (2004): 219-232. For further reference, look at the papers published in the *Journal of the Early Republic*, Vol. 16, No. 2, Special Issue on Capitalism in the Early Republic (Summer, 1996) as well as Douglass C. North, *The Economic Growth of the United States, 1790-1860* (Englewood Cliffs, N.J.: Prentice--Hall, 1961); George Rogers Taylor, *The Transportation Revolution, 1815- 1860* (New York: Routledge, 1951); Gary M. Walton and James F. Sheperd, *The Economic Rise of Early America* (Cambridge, Cambridge University Press, 1979); Howard Bodenhorn, *A History of Banking in Antebellum America: Financial Markets and Economic Development in an Era of Nation-Building* (Cambridge: Cambridge University Press, 2000); Peter Temin, ed., *Engines of Enterprise: An Economic History of New England* (Cambridge, Mass.: Harvard University Press, 2002); Winifred B. Rothenberg, *From Market-Places to a Market Economy: The Transformation of Rural Massachusetts, 1750--1850* (Chicago: University of Chicago Press, 1992); James A. Henretta, *The Origins of American Capitalism: Collected Essays* (Boston: Northeastern University Press, 1991); Allan Kulikoff, *The Agrarian Origins of American Capitalism* (Charlottesville: University Press of Virginia, 1992); Peter A. Coclanis, *The Shadow of a Dream: Economic Life and Death in the South Carolina Low Country, 1670-1920* (New York: Oxford University Press, 1989); In this context, it is also worth looking at the leftist theory of market developments: cf. Barry Clark, *Political Economy: A Comparative Approach* (New York: Preager, 1991); Howard Sherman, *Radical Political Economy: Capitalism and Socialism from a Marxist-Humanist Perspective* (New York: Basic Books, 1972); James F. Becker, *Marxian Political Economy: An Outline* (Cambridge, Cambridge University Press: 1977); Paul M. Sweezy, *The Theory of Capitalist Development: Principles of Marxian Political Economy* (New York: Monthly Review Press, 1942).

[23] Paul Gilje "Rise of Capitalism in the Early Republic," *Journal of the Early Republic* 16.2 (1996): 159-181. Cf. Michael Merrill, "'Cash is Good to Eat': Self-Sufficiency and Exchange in the Rural Economy of the United States," *Radical History Review* 4 (Winter 1977): 42-71; Robert E. Mutch, "Yeoman and Merchant in pre-Industrial America: Eighteenth-century Massachusetts as a Case Study," *Societas* 7 (Autumn 1977): 279-302; Allan Kulikoff, "The Transition to Capitalism in Rural America," *William and Mary Quarterly* 46 (Jan. 1989): 120-144; Christopher Clark, "Economics and Culture: Opening Up the Rural History of the Early American Northeast," *American Quarterly* 43 (June 1991): 279-301; Robert E. Mutch, "Colonial America and the Debate About Transition to Capitalism," *Theory and Society* 9 (Nov. 1980): 847-863; Daniel Vickers, "The Transition to Capitalism in the American Northeast," *History Teacher* 27 (May 1994); 267-269; Thomas S. Wermuth, "Were Early Americans Capitalists? An Overview of the Development of Capitalist Values and Beliefs in Early America," *Mid-America* 74 (Jan. 1992): 85-97; Jeremy Atack and Fred Bateman, *To Their Own Soil: Agriculture in the Antebellum North* (Ames: Iowa State University Press, 1987); Jeremy Atack and Fred Bateman, "Yeoman Farming: Antebellum America's Other 'Peculiar Institution,'"

Republic was the turning point for shaping and defining the elements of modern capitalism. Therefore the market revolution, as some researchers like Charles Sellers or Eric Foner, called these period and events, is essential to present Warren's philosophy in the broader milieu.

New historical approaches led to the conclusion that the agrarian Jeffersonian ideal of yeoman farm life, life that provided a moral anchor, had gradually been fading.[24] At the same time, the idea of work and the value attached to work, so heavily grounded in Puritan tradition, was questioned by the fast profits acquired through speculations.[25]

As Henretta stated, "[t]he tremendous boom in land sales after 1815, especially in the Cotton Belt, brought an equally spectacular increase in the debt owed by farmers and planters to the national government: no less than $23 million dollars by 1819. Even before the financial panic of that year, Congress responded to political pressure, enacting laws in 1818 and again in 1819 that postponed forfeiture for delinquent purchasers.(...) All owners—whether original subscribers or subsequent purchasers, resident farmers or absentee speculators—had the option of taking clear title to the already-paid portion of their property (and relinquishing title to the rest, without paying interest on the arrears) or keeping their entire claim, in which case they could pay it off in eight annual installments, again without interest. As a special incentive, owners who paid off the debt immediately in cash received a discount of no less than 37.5 percent".[26]

The first pivotal point in the market development of the Early Republic was its first spectacular failure—the Panic of 1819. One of the earliest attempts to look at the economy of the early republic was Murray Rothbard's classical piece on the first great American crisis.[27] Rothbard analysed the reasons that caused the crisis, suggesting that the war of 1812 was one of the triggers, contributing to the

---

Agriculture and National Development: Views on the Nineteenth Century, ed. Lou Ferleger (Ames: Iowa State University Press, 1990) 25-51; Hal S. Barron, *Those Who Stayed Behind: Rural Society in Nineteenth-Century New England* (Cambridge: Cambridge University Press, 1984); Christopher Clark, *The Roots of Rural Capitalism: Western Massachusetts, 1780-1860* (Ithaca: Cornell University Press, 1990); James A. Henretta, *The Origins of American Capitalism: Collected Essays* (Boston: Northestern University Press, 1991); Nancy Grey Osterud, "Gender and the Transition to Capitalism in Rural America," *Agricultural History* 67 (Spring 1993): 14-29; Nancy Grey Osterud, "Gender and the Capitalist Transition in Rural America," *History Teacher* 27 (May 1994): 273-76; Bettye Hobbs Pruitt, "Self-Sufficiency and the Agricultural Economy," *William and Mary Quarterly* 41 (July 1984): 333-64.

[24] Henretta, The 'Market' 289-304, also in James A. Henretta, "Families and Farms: Mentalité in Pre-Industrial America," *The William and Mary Quarterly* 35.1 (1987): 3-35; Henretta, *The Origins*; Allen Kulikoff, "The American Revolution, Capitalism, and the Formation of the Yeoman Classes," *Beyond the American Revolution: Explorations in the History of American Radicalism*, Alfred F. Young ed. (DeKalb, Ill: Northern Illinois University Press, 1993) 80-122.

[25] Stephen Aron, "Pioneers and Profiteers: Land Speculation and the Homestead Ethic in Frontier Kentucky," *The Western Historical Quarterly* 23.2 (1992): 179-198.

[26] Henretta, The 'Market' 292-293.

[27] Murray N. Rothbard, *The Panic of 1819: Reactions and Policies* (New York: Columbia University Press, 1962).

crisis either directly, by freezing the foreign trade and stimulating the growth of domestic manufacturing, or indirectly, by creating paper money. In the context of Warren's controversial ideas, we might speculate how much the crisis of 1819 influenced his thought and his personal life. Is it a coincidence that Warren decided to live in Boston and move to the west in a quest for better fortune, or that his family also suffered from the market crash?

In that turbulent times, the major problem to determine was the role that labour should play in human life, not only in the context of the proper reward for it. The question of labour was analysed, redefined and presented in the broader context, it was put in the milieu of sovereignty and individualism. The New England Puritan tradition was built on the Lockean conviction of the importance of labour, that he perceived as the natural right of the individual.[28] On the one hand, labour had this individualistic aspects. As Shively observed, "[u]nder the new system growing up after 1815, a man's occupation became less and less significant. Earlier each man had been a sovereign Individual in a very Lockean sense. Men sold products of their own labor—shoes, pots, hats, almanacs, or bricks—one's labor was a sacred thing—a basic natural right of every man. To sell a man's labor as the new factories required was very much like selling one's soul (...). The threat of lost freedom stimulated men of this period to search for strong bases to insure their independence.(...) The Individualism of Emerson or Thoreau or Jackson or Garrison reaffirmed for these [men] their sense of individual dignity".[29] This emphasises how important for the workers, artisans and merchants of the Early Republic has been the individualism, and at the moment when individualistic and independent character of works was fading they tried to restore it by reaffirming and referring to the notion of individualism on the intellectual level. On the other hand, they sought the communal security provided by the cooperation and cooperative initiatives. "These two strains—strong Individualism and extreme communitarianism—were not necessarily held by different groups of men in society. They could be held by the same men at the same time, for few men are philosophers and even fewer are consistent. Therefore, there is no paradox in the way these men combined contradictor concepts, each of which expressed universal yearnings of mankind".[30]

Shively pointed out that those contradictions were merged and intermingled by the reformers in the early 1800s, this attempt to resolve dichotomy of individualistic and collectivistic approaches to some extent becomes a distinctive element of American attitude. The lack of consistency or the lack of strong attachment to philosophic currents and movements was a result of a strong

---

[28] The first and most classical work showing a correlation between Locke and New England puritans would be the works of Perry Miller, cf. Perry Miller, *The Marrow of Puritan Divinity* (Indianapolis: Bobbs-Merrill, 1937); see also Perry Miller, *The New England Mind: From Colony to Province* (Cambridge: Harvard University Press, 1953), especially 40-52.

[29] Shively, *A Remarkable American* 6-7.

[30] Shively, *A Remarkable American* 7.

practical attitude. Those social reformers and social radicals of early 1800s would experiment and try in practice the various possible options. Therefore, starting from New Harmony – the first secular utopian experiment – all of the pre-Civil War time was marked by numerous social and economic experiments. Using the opportunities offered by westward expansion, those utopian groups led by vision of reform could easily have tested new and more unconventional solutions for social, economic and political problems. Such testing was not perceived as a mere escape from society, but as a valuable way of looking for social progress. In 1840, Emerson, in his letter to Thomas Carlyle, wrote, "[w]e are all a little wild here with numberless projects of social reform. Not a reading man but has a draft of a new community in his waistcoat pocket".[31]

The agrarian Jeffersonian yeoman ideal of a farm life in rural areas was challenged by the new capitalistic entrepreneurial ideas. The major question that an undaunted Jeffersonian[32] had faced would have been how to preserve the broadest possible sphere of individual liberty and the ability of individual actions. As Tucker reminds us, "[t]he study of entrepreneurial history must always have as a focal point the examination of markets and profit maximization. (...) But the history of entrepreneurship cannot be understood without the incorporation of many other areas of inquiry from family dynamics to intergenerational change. (...) And business history reminds us that *homo economicus* is bounded by cultural and moral norms that should be taken into account in an analysis of economic interests and pursuits. The quest for profits and economic efficiency in the early nineteenth century had to be legitimated in the context of a cultural context informed by republican and paternalistic traditions that remained suspicious of, if not fully hostile to, market calculations divorced from moral and familial concerns".[33] Therefore, Warren's experiments should not be described as peculiar and eccentric, but as part of a broader movement, revealing a small fracture in the comprehensive story about how newly-born capitalism transformed the republican ideology.[34]

---

[31] Thomas Carlyle, Ralph W. Emerson, and Charles E. Norton, *The Correspondence of Thomas Carlyle and Ralph Waldo Emerson, 1834-1872* (Boston: J.R. Osgood and Co., 1883) 308.

[32] Later on Benjamin R. Tucker coined and used the term "unterriefied Jeffersonians" to emphasis that the followers of Warren were truthful to revolutionary ideal and carried on the spirit of Early Republic.

[33] Barbara M. Tucker and Kenneth H. Tucker, "The Limits of Homo Economicus: An Appraisal of Early American Entrepreneurship," *Journal of the Early Republic* 24.2 (2004): 217-218.

[34] Stephen J. Ross, "The Transformation of Republican Ideology," *Journal of the Early Republic* 10.3 (1990): 323-330.

CHAPTER 1

RADICAL INDIVIDUALISM
AS UNLABELLED ANARCHY

Individualism, has never been tried. All history, all poetry deal with it only, and because now it was in the minds of men to go alone, and now, before it was tried, now, when a few began to think of the celestial enterprise, sounds this tin trumpet of a French phalanstery, and the newsboys throw up their caps and cry, Egotism is exploded; now for Communism! But all that is valuable in the Phalanstery comes of individualism.

Ralph Waldo Emerson, The Journals and Miscellaneous Notebooks of Ralph Waldo Emerson: 1847-1848 (Cambridge, Mass.: Belknap Press of Harvard Univ. Press) 154.

The main purpose of this chapter is to demonstrate that even though Josiah Warren did not use the term *individualism* in his writings, he was a strong advocate of individuality. Moreover, his individualism was shaped into a radical form that included the notion of the sovereignty of the individual – a notion that was coined and popularised by Warren himself. As a result, Warren rejected the idea of authority being imposed upon individuals. Unwittingly, Warren, who had never used the term *anarchy*, became the first American supporter of anarchism. Anarchy understood as the lack of external constraint was the only acceptable regime and order for him. According to Warren, the only form of political, economic and social relations that enable every individual to keep their right to absolute sovereignty, and to keep the private sphere of the individual free from interference and encroachment, was radical individualism. Although other reasons and theories exist that justify the rejection of political authority, Josiah Warren was the person who developed and popularised the tradition of opposing authority based on the principle of individualism.

1.1. Radical individualism – recovering from the Owenite trauma (the dissolving of combined interests)

1.1.1. Unlabelled individualism

One of the surprising things about Warren is why this man who was one of the earliest, if not the earliest, prophets[35] of individualism avoided the term himself – Warren has never used the term "individualism" in his writing. He preferred instead "individuality" or "separateness of persons". One explanation is the fact that during the 1820s and 1830s – the moment when Warren's philosophical framework was taking shape – the term "individualism" was a novelty. Even more surprising to those who insist that individualism is deeply rooted in the American tradition is the fact that not only the term "individualism" was not commonly used in the early 1800s but it actually had a negative connotation. The first time the term appeared in the United States was in the English translation of Tocqueville's iconic work *Democracy in America.* Tocqueville introduced this term in the following way: "Individualism is a novel expression, to which a novel idea has given birth. (...) Egotism blights the germ of all virtue: Individualism, at first, only saps the virtues of public life; but in the long run, it attacks and destroys all others, and is at length absorbed in downright egotism".[36] Thus, the initial interpretation of this term was highly pejorative. The fact that it appeared in the translation from French indicates not only its foreign origins, but also proves that this novel expression was strange to American culture; culture that already used the notions of self-reliance, self-determination and self-sufficiency to describe itself, and in the early 1800s was not seeking new vocabulary. Koenraad W. Swart points out not only the French origins of this notion, but also the reason for its pejorative connotations. Swart believes that Joseph de Maistre might have invented the term "individualism" to characterise atomisation of society. In a conversation from 1820, de Maistre reportedly referred to excessive fragmentation of all philosophical and political doctrines as a form of "political protestantism carried to the most absolute individualism".[37]

Later on, the term was used by the Saint-Simonians to describe "unsatisfactory mentality resulting from the critical philosophy of the Enlightenment and the French Revolution".[38] There is no evidence that it was used by Saint Simon himself, as he preferred to use the earlier established and popularised terms such as

---

[35] Warren's first writing in which he advocated extreme individuality came from 1827, which is almost a decade before Emerson's writings.

[36] Alexis de Tocqueville, *Democracy in America*, trans. Henry Reeve (Philadelphia: Thomas Cowperthwaite & Co., New York: J. & H. G. Langley, 1840) 104.

[37] Koenrad W. Swart "'Individualism' in the Mid-Nineteenth Century (1826-1860)," *Journal of the History of Ideas* 23.1 (1962): 78. Swart refers to Joseph de Maistre, *Oeuvres Completes* (vol. 14, *Correspondence 1817-1821*, vol. 6 (Lyon: Librairie et Imprimerie Vitte et Perrussel, 1886) 286.

[38] Swart, Individualism 79.

"anarchy" and "egoism".[39] Swart provides evidence that shortly after Saint Simon's death, in 1825, his disciples introduced "individualism" to a broader audience. The first well-established usage of the new term may have been observed in an issue of the periodical *Le Producteur* from 1826, in which the Saint-Simonian P. J. Rouen regretted that the economist Charles Dunoyer, instead of trying to offer an independent, positive solution to contemporary problems, had tried to reduce the new science of the political economy to "the narrow proportions of individualism"[40] characteristic of political philosophy of the eighteenth century.

What is crucially important in Warren's case is another source of pejorative interpretation of the term "individualism" in America. Gregory Claeys associates stigmatisation of the term "individualism" with the activity of Robert Owen, social reformer and father of socialism. In the 1820s and 1830s, first in Great Britain and then in the United States, Owen started to disseminate communal and collective ideas that he perceived as the only desirable form of social relations. Journals like *Circular* and *Pioneer*, organs of Owenite communities, developed and transmitted the negative meaning of individualism, and abound with expressions such as "motives of antipathy and individualism (...) will, in the state of community, be unknown"[41] or "this selfishness, this individualism of action, this disregard of the common good, and exclusive study of partial interests",[42] to point out just some of the examples of individualism's destructive potential.

Admittedly, individuality was at the top of Warren's hierarchy—; the meta-rule that directed all other principles. This motive reappeared in all of his works. The presumption of the importance of individualism led him to the thesis that only the individual is sovereign, and that each individual is his/her own supreme sovereign: "*Every one is by nature constituted to be his or her own government,*

---

[39] Eugène Lerminier asserted in 1831 that Henri Saint-Simon had invented the term *individualism*, but the word has not been found in Saint-Simmon's works, cf. Maxime Leroy, *Histoire des idées sociales en France*, vol. 2 (Paris: Gallimard, 1847) 13, 201.

[40] P. J. Rouen, « Examen de un nouvelle ouvrage de M. Dunoyer Ancien Rédacteur du Censeur Européen » parts 1, *Le Producteur, journal de l'industrie, des sciences et des beaux-arts,* 2, (1826) : 158-170. Especially the passage "Cependant l'individualisme comme base positive de la morale privée a, par cela même, une valeur critique par rapport à la politique; c'est-à-dire, qu'il est le plus puissant adversaire de tous les systèmes vicieux, bien qu'il n'ait point la vertu d'en engendrer un de lui-même. Nous loi devons la destruction de l'ancien ordre social. En effet, la philosophie du xviiiᵉ siècle et des temps précédens démontrait suffisamment que cet ordre social n'était plus qu'un instrument d'oppression, et comprimait en tout sens, le développement des facultés physiques et morales des hommes parvenus a une civilisation plus avancée; elle dévoilait les causes du mal, et bientôt toutes les individualités soulevées contre le système politique, le détruisirent sans retour; mais elles ne possédaient rien encore qui put suffire à réédifier un système nouveau. Ainsi se trouve expliquée celte vérité accueillie et dénaturée parlât passion, que la révolution n'a eu de puissance » Rouen, Examen 162-163.

[41] S. Augustine, "On The Mis-Statement of the St. Simonians On The Subject Of 'Community' To The Editor Of The Pioneer", *Pioneer, or, Grand National Consolidated Trade's Union Magazine* 1 Mar. 1834: 226.

[42] John Brown, "Strikes after strike," *The Crisis, and National Co-operative Trades' Union Gazette* 3 May 1834: 29.

his own law, his own church – each individual is a *system* within himself; and the great problem must be solved with the broadest admission of the *inalienable right of SUPREME INDIVIDUALITY;* which forbids any attempt to *govern* each other, and confines all our legislation to *the adjustment and regulation of our intercourse, or commerce* with each other".[43]

Individuality and the right of the individual to exercise it is the highest law and the highest principle. In Warren's theory, this right was combined with another one, also deeply grounded in American political philosophy – the right to pursue happiness. The philosophical system created and developed by Warren promised all individuals a possibility of self-government and freedom, without the interference from any other power. Proposing the implementation of barter exchange of products and labour, Warren believed that each individual could receive only as much supply of goods as would be necessary for subsistence. As a consequence, the individual could sustain their independence from external interference. Warren constantly repeated this idea: "Out of the indestructibility or inalienability of this Individuality grows the ABSOLUTE RIGHT of its exercise, or the absolute SOVEREIGNTY OF EVERY INDIVIDUAL".[44]

1.1.2. Owenite trauma

Warren and Owen formed a very complex relationship, shaped at least in part by both admiration and contempt (at least on Warren's part). Robert Owen seemed to be indifferent toward Warren's ideas. After the collapse of the New Harmony community he mainly ignored Warren in his publications and speeches.[45] Warren, an important member of the New Harmony community, emerging as the key figure in the movement even at the dusk of the Owenite experiment,[46] expressed his gratitude to his mentor confessing that "I owe it to him that my life is of any value to myself or others. No creature ever heard me utter one word that was disrespectful to Robert Owen and although it is with real pain that I undertake to disconnect his mistakes from that which was true in glorious, I have a right to believe that no man living would more rejoice at my success in this than Robert Owen".[47] At the same

---

[43] Josiah Warren, *Equitable Commerce: A New Development of Principles, as Substitutes for Laws and Governments. Proposed as Elements of New Society* (New Harmony: published by the author, 1846) 4-5. All emphasis in Warren's quotations as original if not stated otherwise.

[44] Josiah Warren, *Equitable Commerce: A New Development of Principles As Substitutes for Laws and Governments... Proposed As Elements of New Society* (New York: Fowlers and Wells, 1852) 18.

[45] To verify to what extent Warren was ignored after his departure from communal ideals by Robert Owen, it is essential to investigate Owen's family papers; however, the majority of them are not currently available to researchers.

[46] His signature appeared on the legal document—a lease titled "Education Society to Robert Owen" and dated August 24, 1826—referring to land to be used for the establishment of an iron foundry, cf. Josephine Elliott, "The Owen Family Papers," *Indiana Magazine of History* 60.4 (1964): 335-336.

[47] Josiah Warren, *Notes*, Folder 13: Lecture and Notes, Box 1. Josiah Warren Papers, Labadie Collection, Special Collections Library, University of Michigan. Besides these declarations, there is

time, the core elements of Warren's system: an appraisal for individuality, a call for individual private ownership as well as a strong condemnation of unification, uniformisation and the communal form of life – stood in complete opposition to what Robert Owen intended to implement in his projects.

The social experiment in New Harmony was important not only because it became a formative experience for Warren, but it also had a tremendous impact on the process of shaping and developing Warren's philosophical system. Even though it lasted a relatively short time (1825-1827), this community was the most popular and had the most far reaching consequences among other communities, and it has been the turning point for Warren's intellectual development. For this project, Owen used the space previously occupied by the Rapp community (also called the Harmony Society or the Harmonists). Owen purchased the land with the building from Rappites in 1824[48] and gathered around himself between 800 and 900 people turning the community into one of the biggest utopian experiments.[49]

Owen stated his goal clearly when he said: "I come to this country, to introduce an entire new state of society; to change it from the ignorant, selfish system, to an enlightened, social system, which shall gradually unite all interests into one, and remove all cause for contest between individuals. (...) change from the individual to the social system; from single families with separate interests, to communities of many families with one interest".[50] Owen suggested among other

---

no evidence that such a feeling was mutual. Robert Owen rarely mentioned Josiah Warren. There is also no written evidence that Owen "rejoiced" at Warren's successes. Warren firmly stated that his main reason was to "undertake to disconnect his mistakes from that which was true in glorious". It is essential to keep in mind that the process of disconnection had a radical character. No matter what Warren publicly declared, he built up his entire philosophical system in opposition to Owen's communal ideas.

[48] Edward K. Spann, *Brotherly Tomorrows: Movements for a Cooperative Society in America, 1820-1920* (New York: Columbia University Press, 1989) 16.

[49] Noyes, *American Socialism* 15-16. More on this experiment see George. B. Lockwood, *The New Harmony Movement* (New York: D. Appleton and Co, 1905); Arthur E. Bestor Jr., *Backwoods Utopias: The Sectarian Origins and Owenite Phases of Communitarian Socialism in America, 1663– 1829* (Philadelphia: University of Pennsylvania Press, 1971); William Alfred Hinds, *American Communities and Co-operative Colonies* (Chicago: Charles H. Kerr & Co, 1908) ; Roger S. Fogarty, *Dictionary of American Communal History* (Westport: Greenwood Press, 1980); J. F. C. Harrison, *Robert Owen and the Owenites in Britain and America: Quest for the New Moral World* (New York: Charles Scribner's Sons, 1969); Seymour R. Kesten, *Utopian Episodes: Daily Life in Experimental Colonies Dedicated to Changing the World* (Syracuse N.Y.: Syracuse University Press, 1993); Roger P. Sutton, *Communal Utopias and the American Experience: Secular Communities, 1824-2000* (Westport: Praeger Publishers, 2004); Donald E. Carmony, Josephine M. Elliott, "New Harmony, Indiana: Robert Owen's Seedbed for Utopia," *Indiana Magazine of History* 76.3 (Sept. 1980): 161-261; Mark Holloway, *Heavens on Earth Utopian Communities in America 1680-1880* (London: Turnstiles Press, 1951) 101-116; Edward K. Spann, *Brotherly Tomorrows: Movements for a Cooperative Society in America, 1820-1920* (New York: Columbia University Press, 1989) 17-49. I want to express my gratitude to professor Hartmut Kliemt for drawing my attention to Hinds.

[50] "Address; Delivered by Robert Owen of New Lanark," *New Harmony Gazette* 1 Oct. 1825: 1.

things, that education would lead to reduced competitiveness and harmonious cooperation.[51]

An observer of the collapse of the New Harmony experiment, Warren published a detailed analysis of the events in the *Western Tiller*. It was published anonymously *"by a late member of New Harmony"* and entitled "To the Friends of the Social System". Warren mentioned his own *Time Store* experiment that he had run at that time in Cincinnati, a fact that helps us identify him as the author. His publications during the years 1827 and 1828 suggest that the core of his philosophical theories had been fully shaped, introducing a system with exceptional coherence. Later, Warren used numerous eclectic references trying to explain or provide additional support for his intellectual framework. But when we take into consideration that in early 1827 his ideas were already so fully shaped and developed, it becomes clear that his thinking was largely independent and developed earlier than that of other writers he referred to. His individualism preceded both Emerson's and Johnson's writings, and his hostility towards the government anticipated Proudhon's. Thus Warren, is a remarkable example of an intellectual self-made man who created his ideas independently, without borrowing from others.

He explained the reasons for New Harmony's failure in the following passage: "This hasty and unexpected assemblage of persons from all parts of the earth so widely different from each other, without any previous preparation for business, or for domestic accommodations, could not but produce confusion and counteraction at almost every step. Each one had his peculiar habits of thinking, which had been produced by his *particular circumstances*, so that we were continually crossing each other at all points. Mr. Owen appeared to design that we should learn our great lesson by *experience*; well knowing that in matters of importance, we cannot safely trust to any other instructor. Therefore, he encouraged every trial of government, and every species of arrangement for which we exhibited any inclination, and I believe that a faithful trial has been made of almost all things of that nature. Laws and regulation were adopted which, at the time of making them appeared quite unexceptionable in every respect; but in practice we found that instead of facilitating they only retarded our progress".[52] Warren noticed that individuality led people to various and different interpretations, while Owen expected unanimity. According to Warren, such harmony was impossible while "[e]ach person constructed (...)[laws and regulations] according to his own peculiar ideas, which were effects of his own peculiar circumstances, and this difference gave rise to long and tedious controversies, which of course differ from

---

[51] "The Constitution of the Preliminary Society of New Harmony (The Society is instituted generally to promote the Happiness of the World" *New Harmony Gazette* 1 Oct. 1825: 2-3; Paul Brown, *Twelve Months in New-Harmony: Presenting a Faithful Account of the Principal Occurrences Which Have Taken Place There Within That Period; Interspersed with Remarks* (Cincinnati: W.H. Woodward, 1827) 23-28; Carmony, Elliott, New Harmony 169-179.

[52] Josiah Warren, "To the Friends of Social System no. 1," *Western Tiller* 1 June 1827: 2.

the same cause. This generally ended in a revolution of government or change of laws, which immediately followed by the same effects. So constant and unceasing was this state of things, that, confused, disappointed and discouraged many of our valuable friends left us with the impression that the system was impracticable, or inapplicable to the present age".[53]

Later, in the early 1830s Warren turned his attention to the epistemological aspects of human understanding. Different people have different senses and therefore different cognitive abilities. Warren was also very interested in the linguistic aspects of human co-operation and in the difficulties of the notion of communication between people.[54] He observed that "[t]hus did this simple language of Mr. Owen produce almost as many different conclusions as there were individuals who heard it. The general observer referred it to all human thoughts, feelings and actions and attributed this difference to the different *causes* which had acted upon each individual, and therefore attached neither merit to themselves nor demerit to those who differed from them; and upon this knowledge, *Individual Liberty* was so far established: but it was established only with a few, and with them, in the mind only. Our surrounding institutions, customs and public opinion call for *conformity:* they require us to act in masses like herds of cattle: they do not recognise the fact that we think and feel *individually* and ought to be at liberty to act individually; but this liberty cannot be enjoyed in combinations, masses and connections in which one cannot move without affecting another".[55] Warren was certain that using any names that referred to the general feellings, thoughts and actions was inappropriate epistemologically. People acknowledge and understand the world only as individuals. This approach was also reflected in Warren's fascination with language, and the ways different people ascribed different meanings to the same words.

Warren's diagnosis remained unchanged; three decades later, he still saw this artificial unity as the main reason for the collapse of New Harmony. Warren revealed that: "[w]e had assured ourselves of our unanimous devotedness to the cause and expected unanimity of thought and action: but instead of this we met diversity of opinions, expedients and counteraction entirely beyond any thing we had just left behind us in common society: and the more we desired and called for "union" the more this diversity seemed to be developed: and instead of that harmonious co-operative we had expected, we found more antagonisms than we had been accustomed to in common Life. (...) We differed, we contended and ran ourselves into confusion: our legislative proceedings were just like all others (...) We had fairly worn each other out by incessant legislation about organizations, constitutions, laws and regulations all to no purpose, and we could no longer

---

[53] Warren, To the Friends of Social System (1 Jun 1827): 2.

[54] This explains why later on, in the early 1830s, Warren became so fascinated with the writings of A.B Johnson on language.

[55] Josiah Warren, "Individuality," *Peaceful Revolutionist* 1.4. (April 5th 1833): 13.

talk with each other on the subject that brought us there. Many intelligent and far seeing members had left—others were preparing to go, and an oppressive dispondency hung heavily upon all".[56] This view was shared by others, including William Maclure: "Even with persons brought up from childhood to act in common and live in common, it would be impossible to carry out a communistic system, unless in a place utterly removed from contact with the world".[57]

Observing the fall of New Harmony Warren provided similar diagnosis: "*imaginary* masses, for, notwithstanding that the ingenuity of man has been exerted to the utmost, and that interest, fears, hopes, persuasion fraud and force have been brought to bear upon human motives to make men think, feel, decide and act alike; and ages have passed away in witnessing and suffering the calamitous consequences, yet, at this late day, it remains for us to attract attention to the *INDIVIDUALITY OF CHARACTER* observable throughout the human race- to *the various effects which the same circumstance produces upon persons whose previous circumstances have been different, and, to the different effects produced by the same circumstance upon the same person at different times.* This *individuality of persons and cases,* no power within our knowledge can destroy or control; and the facts that 'no one has any power to like that which is disagreeable' and that every one is compelled to like that which is agreeable" teach us, as we love our own happiness, to respect every one's individual feelings and Liberty, and not to make any social arrangements which compel us to violate them".[58]

When we look at Warren's endeavour towards individualism, it is quite evident that he saw it as the only remedy for forced unanimity. It is hard to overestimate the importance of the time Warren spent in New Harmony and there is no doubt that it had had shaped his entire philosophical system. Analysing what happened, William Bailie wrote that "...through all the vicissitudes, disappointments, and failures of the community during two stormy years, Warren remained and bore his share of the burdens incident to so pretentious an undertaking. Not as an embittered reactionary, however, did he finally take his leave, but as an earnest and hopeful student who had spent his time to good purpose, one who, through witnessing the inadequacy of communism to correct the evils of private property, and the failure of both paternal authority and majority rule as forms of government, had learned his lessons and stored up pregnant experiences for use in future efforts to elucidate the same vital issue".[59]

---

[56] Josiah Warren, "Untitled", *The Quarterly Letter: Devoted Mainly to Showing the Practical Applications and Progress of "Equity"* (October 1867): 2.

[57] Noyes, *American* 50, cf. William L. Sargant, *Robert Owen and His Social Philosophy* (London: Smith and Elder, 1860) 252-254.

[58] Josiah Warren, "Untitled", *Peaceful Revolutionist*, 1.2 (Feb. 1833): 6.

[59] William Bailie, *Josiah Warren: The First American Anarchist* (Boston: Small, Maynard & Co., 1906) 4-5.

1.1.3. Separateness of all[60]

Already in his earliest publication in *Western Tiller*, Warren observed that the world is complex, built on differences, and any attempt to generalise the experience of our senses would be futile. "One says," he pointed out "it is true that no two are alike, and it is true that we cannot at all times feel alike; nor can we always desire the same treatment, the same company, the same subjects for contemplation, the same air, the same place, be it ever agreeable as a change; nor can we desire for a long time the same sensations of any kind".[61] He returned to the idea in 1833, when he stated that "Nothing is more common than such remarks as the following. 'No two things are alike' 'There can be no rules without exceptions' &c. yet, we are constantly called upon to conform to rules that do not suit our case, to acquiesce in numerous different opinions all at the same moment, and no laws in the world preserve the liberty of the governed to make exceptions to the rules which they are required to obey; but, to give others the power to construe laws and make exceptions, is equivalent to giving them the power to govern without laws. A little observation will disclose an *Individuality* in persons, times, and circumstances which has suggested the idea, that one of our most fatal errors has been the laying down rules, laws, and principles without preserving the liberty of each person to apply them according to the individuality of his views, and the circumstances of different cases: in other words, our error, like that of all the world that has gone before us has been, the violation of individual Liberty".[62]

His beliefs about diversity and lack of unanimity were additionally supported by the linguistic writings of Alexander Bryan Johnson. Warren referred to them twice in the surviving issues of "Peaceful Revolutionist", for the first time in February 1833, when he promised "...to illustrate there important subjects more fully in future numbers, but for a most clear and satisfactory view of the nature of language to which I have allude, see Alex'r. B. Johnson's 'Philosophy of human

---

[60] Crispin Sartwell in his *Practical Anarchist* provided the deepest and most brilliant observation of Warren's individualism showing how extraordinary Warren's attitude was. Sartwell also drew the parallel between Warren's standpoint and Heraclitan atomism. This is one of the most creative perspectives that has been offered. When I first read the *Peaceful Revolutionist*, I saw a great similarity between Warren's view and the Aristotelian movement from particularities to universalities. However, Warren decided to stop his quest and analysis at the level of particularities, and did not search for any universal element refusing to believe that such universalities existed. As a result of such premises, Warren did not look for what different things and people might have in common, perceiving such a quest as pathological and highly destructive. However, after consideration, I found Sartwell attempts to compare Warren and Heraclid more appealing than tracing similarities between Warren and Aristotle. I am also highly indebted to Sartwell's analysis of the role that A.B. Johnson might have played as the source of inspiration for Warren's individualism. It should be emphasised that Corrine Jacker was the first scholar to point out Johnson's impact on Warren; cf. Corrine Jacker, *The Black Flag of Anarchy: Antistatism in the United States* (New York: Charles Scribner's Sons, 1968) 55.

[61] Warren, To the friends of Social System (22 June 1827): 2.

[62] Josiah Warren, "Individuality," *Peaceful Revolutionist* 5 Apr. 1833: 13.

knowledge, or lectures on language' delivered at the lyceum at Utica, NY. This work, instead of being the last to make disappearance, should [I think] have been the first; especially, to legislators. And why it has not found its way into the hands of every individual in society, I can only account for by the fact that it most effectually detects those subtleties and dissolves those delusions of language by which the uniformed have for ages been tricked out of their property and liberty. I regret the necessity of this harsh construction of appearances, but surrounding cannibalism admits no other, and these harsh conclusions and bad feelings cannot cease until some portions of society cease to live upon others".[63]

From Johnson's treaty, published in 1828, it is clear that the author was perfectly aware of the inability of language to fully describe their surroundings to human beings: "[a] perfect language should have a separate word for each of these appearances, and a separate word for every other phenomenon; but a language thus precise would be too copious for our memory: hence in every tongue the same word is applied to many phenomena. This versatility of language produces little embarrassment in the ordinary concerns of life, but in speculation it occasions controversy and confusion. When a metaphysician discovers that a word is appropriated to discordant existences, he supposes that the disagreement is an anomaly in nature, instead of a property of language".[64] Possibly inspired by this passage, Warren reached the conclusion that each individual should have a right to personal interpretation, without being forced into uniformity of understanding and defining concepts.

Warren's second reference to Johnson's work was in April 1833 when he openly admitted that his perception of individuality "... is a continuation of [Johnson's] invaluable labors on language (...). [W]ithout hesitation acknowledge the benefit I have derived from Mr. J's 'Lectures on Language' (...). [L]et me here inform my readers that I use language with a constant regard to its principles as developed by Mr. Johnson. Enquirers will thus always have a key to my meaning, and opposers (should I have them) may save themselves much labor by studying his work as I do not intend to enter into any argument where the language does not refer to some sensible 'phenomena'. Mr. Johnson's elucidation of language is a bridge over which I have escaped from the bewildering labyrinths of verbal delusions called arguments and controversies, and I do not expect to recross it but as a free child of a peaceful village would approach the uproar and confusion of a noisy city on a holiday in pursuit of variety".[65]

Acknowledging an inability to find and communicate what some called universality, Warren ended up questing for particularities: "It looks back to and elaborates the classical empiricists and common sense philosophers in one

---

[63]   Josiah Warren, "Society as it is," *Peaceful Revolutionist* 1.2 (Feb. 1833): 8.
[64]   Alexander B. Johnson, *The Philosophy of Human Knowledge; or, A Treatise on Language: A Course of Lectures Delivered at the Utica Lyceum* (New York: G. & C. Carvill, 1828) 56-57.
[65]   Warren, Individuality 13.

direction and strikingly anticipates logical positivism and pragmatism on the other. For Johnson, the meaning of a statement or theory is the means that would be used to prove or give evidence for it; a statement means the difference it would practically make in experience. He attacked language on grounds that might be termed radically nominalistic. Nature, he said, appeared only in particulars, whereas the words applied to these particulars were always general. That is, in every instance of a different thing to which a word refers or which falls into its extension, the same word is applied, but in each case the particular phenomenon is distinct. This leads philosophers and the rest of us into a massively fallacious interpretation of nature, in which it is viewed as a series of instantiations of universals. Rather, language should be adapted to the ever-more-precise delineation of particulars".[66] But as Corrin Jacker observed, in Warren's case, his opinions about semiotics influenced his perception of governmental and legal order, or rather the rejection of the possibility of establishing such governmental or legal order on a non-individualistic level. For Warren, any commonly shared interpretation of law was imbued with a violent element. It imposed upon the individual the fixed and artificial interpretation of legal rules. Thus, when Warren "...began at this time to study the semantics theories of Alexander Bryan Johnson, what he learned gave him new arguments for his feelings about the oppressiveness of the State. Warren began to argue that government and law were not material objects, but rather forms of language. Since this was so, like any word structures, they could be defined in different ways by different persons, and then interpreted and put into effect accordingly".[67]

The study of semiotics led Warren to deny an externally imposed generalisation – done either by authority or by law – but it also provided an additional impulse to adopt a radically individual perspective in organising his social experiment and presenting it to others not as a generalisation but as the sum of individual testimonies and statements. Writing to Robert Dale Owen in 1831 he stated: "I speak often of myself, I offer my apology in the fact that we have a distinct understanding that whatever we do is done entirely in the individual character, each taking on himself all the responsibility of his own actions. There is no combination whatever among us; the personal liberty of each is considered sacred, and I shall therefore not use the term we, nor speak of others except in cases where the free choice of each individual concerned has been consulted".[68] Unfortunately, there is no written evidence that Warren was acquainted with Johnson's work published in 1836 – *A Treatise on Language: Or, the Relation Which Words Bear to Things, in Four Parts*, the work that seems even more co-aligned with Warren's ideas. Johnson stated that "[i]ndividuality is no anomaly of nature. It is nature's regular production, and boundless richness (...) No two parcels of calomel possess the

---

[66] Sartwell, *Practical Anarchist* 27-28.
[67] Jacker, *The Black Flag* 55.
[68] J. W. [Josiah Warren], "Social Experiment," *Free Enquirer* 26 Feb. 1831: 137.

perfect identity which the sameness of their name implies. No two men possess the perfect identity which the sameness of their manhood implies; nor possesses any one man, at all times, and under all circumstances, the complete identity with which language invests his individuality".[69] Some passages in Warren's work indicates that he might have also been inspired by this later work of Johnson's when in 1852 he stated that "[t]he false step is in laying down any verbal laws, rules, or propositions of any kind which embrace any conditions not distinctly seen, appreciated, and voluntarily consented to by the entering parties, and in adopting any language in the shape of rules, or laws, or institutions, which admits of more than one *individual* interpretation; but as no laws or articles of compact, embracing so many particulars and so wide a range, can be made thus definite, *language is unfit for the basis of social organization or political institutions*".[70]

In his first book entitled *Equitable Commerce*, when Warren introduced the purpose of his writing and the reason behind his method of research and study, he openly admitted that the book was dedicated to "*THE STUDY OF INDIVIDUALITY, or the practice of mentally discriminating, dividing, separating, disconnecting persons, things, and events, according to their individual peculiarities*".[71] Only the separation of interests and adoption of an individual perspective allow people to solve social problems. "Let all interests to be '*individualized*' and we have remedy required. Let there be no national or state business; let the post office be conducted like mercantile interests by individual; let the circulating medium be issued by individuals like bills of exchange, railroad tickets, or omnibus tickets, theater tickets, &c. Let the miscellaneous intercourse of nations be conducted on *individual responsibilities*, instead of as now *on National responsibilities...*".[72]

For Warren, it was important that this call to acknowledge individuality included not only adults, but was introduced as part of an educational process and applied to children as well. He stated repeatedly that parents should "p l a c e t h e i r c h i l d r e n u p o n t h e i r o w n s e p a r a t e a n d d i s t i n c t i n t e r e s t s, entirely separate and distinct from the interests of parents or masters or rulers— in other words let all mankind learn. Individuality!!!".[73]

---

[69] Alexander B. Johnson, *A Treatise on Language: Or, the Relation Which Words Bear to Things, in Four Parts* (New York: Harper & brothers, 1836) 67.

[70] Josiah Warren and Stephen P. Andrews, *Practical Details in Equitable Commerce: Showing the Workings, in Actual Experiment, During a Series of Years, of the Social Principles Expounded in the Works Called "Equitable Commerce," by the Author of this, and "The Science of Society" by Stephen P. Andrews. Volume 1.* (New York: Fowles and Wells, 1852) 78-79.

[71] Warren, *Equitable Commerce* (1846) 3.

[72] Josiah Warren, "Untitled," *Periodical Letter* 1.5, 2nd series (July 1857): 67.

[73] Josiah Warren, *Notebook D*, Working Men's Institute Libraries, original emphasis, kept as in the manuscript, unpaginated. The original manuscript can be found in the Working Men's Institute in New Harmony. Warren's notebook is unpaginated, therefore all the page numbers refer to the typescript prepared as part of the master thesis by Ann C. Butler. On the last page of Notebook D there is information suggesting that other notebooks were labelled by letters A to J. According to oral information obtained from Lynnman Warren, one of Warren's descendants, other notebooks

As Sartwell summarised it, "[i]n application to human beings, Warren's particularism takes the form of an affirmation of the irreducibility of subjectivity and a critique of language, in particular written language. For Warren, the problem at the heart of a political order is that it necessarily de-individualizes its subjects, treating them en masse or in classes. In his view, the worst imaginable approach would be to subject human beings to laws or constitutions, which are inevitably interpreted differently by each person, or even by the same person at different times. To freeze a dynamic social order into a document is mere folly: you simply launch into the interminable, and in principle insoluble, process of interpretation. Words are the tools of persons (...), and that cannot be changed until human subjectivity can be eradicated. The eradication of subjectivity (...) would be the eradication of persons and the world they experience. In other words, subjectivity is a dimension of the massed specificities of each person, a human aspect of the pluralism and dynamism of the universe. Indeed, the political movement of modernity, which depends in almost any of its formulas on some system of combining interests and identities, is according to Warren—simply a fantasy and a recipe for interminable conflict. In his view, people clash when their interests are the same, not when they are carefully distinguished, and conflict can be minimized by extricating people from one another, not by rolling them up in ever-larger human bales".[74]

According to Warren separateness of everything was the only guarantee for Liberty, "*Liberty, therefore, can not exist until all combinations and united interests are dissolved back again into* INDIVIDUALITIES. When this is done, and each is acknowledged SOVEREIGN OF HIMSELF AND HIS OWN, then we shall have a definition of Liberty, and more, for we shall have *Liberty itself*".[75]

This principle was related to the freedom of the press and the right to publish whatever a person would like to publish. However, this freedom of speech and dissemination of ideas was merely a different form of axiological neutrality. In other words, Warren openly admits that the expression of convictions and opinions could be accepted only on a personal, individual level. Therefore, "Liberty of the press is the freedom to print whatever I like to have printed, and so with every one else. This accords with our natural *Individualities;* and (in the progressive stage of society) we shall differ; but we have no liberty to differ in combinations; one way or another must prevail *for all. We can differ only in proportion as we and our interests are individualized*, consequently *Individualization*, instead of '*combining*' is the first step in progress! This is directly contrary to all societary formations, and all the formulas for life-formations. 'True religion' is *my* individual religion, and so with every one else's. No two have precisely the same conception of it! The recognition of the inherent right of individuality is the only harmonizer. True morality is my particular morality; true virtue is my virtue; sound reason

were destroyed by Warren's son George probably right after his father's demise. Cf. Ann C. Butler, *Josiah Warren, Peaceful Revolutionist*, diss., Ball State University 1978, (UMI 7919881) 36.

[74] Sartwel, *Practical Anarchist* 7-8.
[75] Warren, Andrews, *Practical Details* (1852) 83.

is my particular reasoning; 'the highest grade of intelligence' is my particular intelligence; and all this is equally true, relatively, of every other individual. The idea of any one standard must be given up, and every one be allowed to be his own standard, before we shall take the first step toward harmonious adjustment".[76]

1.2. Individual choices – collective decisions?

1.2.1. Cooperating individuals – non-atomistic reality

Considering Warren's level of individualism, the major concern was how people inhabiting the world he envisioned could co-exist and live and work together. What would prevent them from descending into atomism or even solipsism? What did people in Warren's vision have in common? The solution was the pursuit of happiness. "I find myself placed in the company [of] other human beings, all of whom appear to differ from each other, and I perceive myself to differ from all the rest; and I perceive that I cannot at all times feel the same sensations, or be influenced by the same thoughts; but that my thoughts change, and my sensations become agreeable or disagreeable according, to the multifarious combinations of circumstances that produce them. Therefore, as I desire my own happiness at all times. I wish to have the power in all cases, and in all situations, of **DICTATING MY OWN CIRCUMSTANCES IN EVERY RESPECT, AND IN EVERY POINT OF VIEW;** and I am anxious that all others may enjoy the same security, in order that we may no longer counteract each other, but that we may render and receive assistance in our pursuit of happiness. Perceiving that I cannot control my sensations, I wish to have power sufficient to control the causes which produce them. I wish to retain and secure all those causes which are capable of producing agreeable sensations, and to avoid or remove all those which produce unhappiness. In doing this I require the assistance of others; therefore, I invite all those who have similar desires to make them known, in order that I may have an opportunity of assisting them, and thereby of creating in them a disposition to render me their assistance in return. This constitution or instrument will appear new, and perhaps singular, to those who have not been influenced by the same train of thought which dictated it; but upon reflection it will be perceived in our intercourse with each other; that by referring to that, we shall refer to the laws of our own nature, instead of the laws of men".[77]

The need for co-operation, according to Warren, was grounded in people's strive for happiness that could not be achieved without the assistance of others. Warren, thought that this tendency worked on two different levels. On the first level, the quest for happiness and avoidance of unhappiness seemed almost subconscious, as they were based on sensual experience. "Always referring to the

---

[76] Warren, Andrews, *Practical Details* (1852) 82.
[77] Warren, To the Friends of Social System (1 June 1827): 2.

fact, that *we are the creatures of the circumstances that surround us*,[78] we analyze the combination of every moment, and find in each some that differ from all others, but one which is always the same, which determines every action, and which nothing can every control; this is, *my desire of happiness*; it is the first circumstance in point of importance; it is the once in comparison to which, all others sing into insignificance; it is the once which induces me to change and to modify all others to accommodate it. It is an itself *omnipotent*, and I have no power whatever to control it; my only business seems to be to obey its dictates without demur; whatever stands in its way, it bids me avoid – whatever pleases it, it bids me cherish".[79] On the other level, there was an intellectual component of searching for happiness, and happiness itself was not defined in a merely hedonistic manner but rather in the long term perspective, thinking and evaluating consequences of human's actions. When Warren thought of whiskey, "the circumstance of association presents to [his] mind human misery, in every shape; intoxicated men, despairing mothers, ragged starving children, pilfering, want, officers, laws, trials, convictions, dungeons and death. These are circumstances over which I have no control, and my **desire of happiness** bids me avoid them".[80]

Therefore in this sense his vision was not exclusively based on self-perfection and moderation. In co-existing with other people, Warren demanded not only the respect of the sphere of rights, but also a broadly understood sphere of privacy; he stressed the importance of abstaining form advising others about their lives as this could lead to hostility and jeopardise future chances for receiving assistance in one's strive for happiness. Then quite often "there are circumstances with which *advice* and *instruction* are at present connected, in such a manner, that their utility is lost, and their object defeated. For instance, my instructors sometimes unluckily take such *times* and *places* to advise me, that it very often interrupts my pursuit of some other object; and it non unfrequently happens while we are in the presence of other company, that I must either engage in arguments of defence, or submit to a display of their acquirements at the expense of my own; either of which is disagreeable when I am in the company of those whose good opinion I am anxious to retain ; therefore let me 'dictate' my own *time* and *place* for instruction and advice. Persons generally have not been in the habit of *giving* me advice and instruction, unless it was in some manner to promote their own happiness, or when I have unfortunately interfered with it; and then advice was so nearly connected with reproof or dictation, that I sought rather to *defend* than to *reform* myself. But let all others for the present and future feel themselves *secure* from my *interference* and of my assistance; and then when I hear advice or instruction, I shall suspect that it is for my own good".[81]

---

[78] This passage offers a clear reminiscence of Owen's theory.
[79] Warren, To the Friends of the Social System (8 June 1827): 2.
[80] Warren, To the Friends of the Social System (8 June 1827): 2.
[81] Warren, To the Friends of the Social System (15 June 1827): 2.

In 1840, for the first time Warren collected all expectations and demands that he felt were necessary for the functioning of his system:

"1. ...proceedings are conducted with a watchful and strict regard to the laws of our nature. Particularly its Individualities. (...)

3. n o t t o make any Social Arrangements which require compulsion, or the violation of the natural liberty of the individual

4. Not to make such as depend for their success upon the coincidence of opinions, tastes or interests but to preserve the liberty of each to differ in all these and all other respects,

5. and the liberty to c h a n g e with his situation.

6. This natural liberty being; impracticable in combinations, masses and organized associations having connected interests, & connected responsibilities, we are hereby taught n o t t o f o r t h e m; but to preserve

7. Individual Interests

8. Individual Responsibilities

9. Individual Executives or

10. The sovereignty of every individual over his or her person, time and property".[82]

1.2.2. Between individual choices and collective rules

Among the advocates of radical liberty one of the most popular questions was that of the transformation of individual choices into a collective decision-making process. They wondered whether there was any guarantee or mechanism that would ensure that an individual decision led to collective choices. Or was there a way to encourage certain desirable patterns of behaviour, and what would motivate individuals to change their mind to embrace such patterns? Could people recognise individual laws that could be binding patterns? Was there a form of social cooperation that would allow people to create community, or adopt some form of social contract, while at the same time allowing them to retain their individual rights, keeping their sovereignty intact? In an interview for the *New York Sentinel*, the publication's editor quoted an anonymous witness who wrote that "The principle advocated by our Cincinnati informant seem to us, (from a cursory view of it,) at once more practicable, and more in accordance with the spirit of individual freedom. He proposes no association, no society, no general rules to apply to all characters, however dissimilar, and to all tastes, however opposed. He proposes only, that, by gradual and voluntary consent, men should agree, in all their commercial intercourse with each other, to buy, sell, barter or exchange, *on the principle of labor for equal labor*".[83] Thus, according to this writer, not only was such a phenomenon possible, but it already existed, enacted through Warren's

---

[82] Josiah Warren, *Notebook D* 3-4.
[83] "Equal Exchange of Labor," *New York Sentinel and Working Man's Advocate* 17 July 1830: 1.

experiment. Given that view, it is, therefore, essential to examine closely the daily activities of the members of Warren's experiment in an attempt to trace evidence that their individual choices and decisions had an impact on a collective/social level. In case of individual anarchy such as envisioned by Warren and assuming the absence of any external power as well as authority, the collective good and collective choices would be just the sum of individual decisions and individual flourishing, and nothing else would then be necessary to function within society (if such a construct as the sum of individuals could even be called *society*). The boundaries of individual freedom would not be infringed, because there would be no possibility of using the argument of acting on behalf of the common good.

Warren, who lived as he preached and respected individualism and independence of the members of his social experiments, was not a typical leader of a utopian community; he was not a charismatic speaker neither was he a guru who imposed strict rules upon his followers. Such attitude resulted in a very loose structure of Warren's social and economic experiments. For that reason these experiments being highly inclusive and open. Warren's refusal to impose any form of structural frame on any of his communities or even his hostility towards any such attempts were grounded in the conviction, later shared by many anarchists, that human nature is good. This loose structure reflected the principle of the sovereignty of the individual. According to this principle Warren thought that each individual had ultimate control of his or her decisions, and as long as he or she was willing to participate in such experiment individuals would act based on no harm principle. So any action will be permitted as long as the action taker is the sole bearer of its action consequences. People would be guided by this *decorum* and based on it they would voluntarily refrain from any action that might harm others. Joining any collective would mean, according to Warren, a tacit agreement to accept the rules that governed its members. Warren used the example of the smoking prohibition in public rooms, observing that "whoever enters does so in accordance with his own free choice, and knows that, as long as he refrains from smoking cigars, he will be at peace".[84] On the other hand, "if it be made a rule that whoever enters there will be required to contribute to general order and decorum, this would be an indefinite rule and he might think himself hereby elected co-superintendent of the movements of everyone in the room".[85]

From its inception, Warren's utopian vision faced the problem of those who were not bound by the concept of *decorum* and proper behaviour, understood as the non-coercion principle. Charles Codman, one of the members of the Modern Times community, wrote in the manuscript related to the history of the colony that "[t]he fundamental mistake that we made, was in thinking that even a small per cent of those who are clamorous and insistent for Justice are honest and in earnest – they are not, and in sadness I write it, they want to pray and shout for it,

---

[84] Warren, *Notebook D* 110.
[85] Warren, *Notebook D* 111.

but are far from ready to practice".[86] Codman's statement suggests that among the inhabitants of Warren's communities there were also those who did not follow the unwritten and vague rules. The classical question of political philosophy is what to do with violators of order. Warren did not pause to ask that question, motivated perhaps by his optimistic belief that human beings were good by nature. Warren believed that all members of his experiment would follow the norms and respect the sovereignty of others as a form of reciprocity to those already respecting their sovereignty.

There is very little evidence about practical violations and encroachments upon individual sovereignty committed by the members of the Utopia or Tuscarowa communities. It is hard to determine whether such absence of evidence was a result of the fact that both communities were extremely small with social pressure and control of an individual's actions being stronger or that the communities were so short-lived that their members had dispersed before a conflicting situation occurred. The best documented case is that of the Modern Times. This community was located on Long Island; its closeness to New York City attracted considerable number of eccentrics and adventure seekers, rather than committed followers of Warren's principles. After reports appeared in the *New York Daily Tribune* advertising the Modern Times' colony, the flow of such people became even more intense. As Warren, after many years, complained: "The effect was, a rush of people, ignorant of the principles upon which the enterprise was projected: among these were some that were full of 'crotchets!'—each one seeming to think that the salvation of the world depended on his displaying his particular hobby. One regular impostor travelled over the Island announcing *himself as* the founder of the village; and he put forth such crude theories, especially with regard to Marriage, that his audiences were disgusted, not only with, him, but with what they supposed the village to be; and some very good neighbors who had kindly welcomed us to the neighborhood, shut their doors in the face of one who was offering them hand bills to counteract the blasting influence of this lying impostor".[87]

In his writing, Warren discussed a few cases that involved violators of the order. Surprisingly, all of these cases related to instances of nudity. As Warren commented: "[a]nother favorite crotchet of his was, that children ought to be brought up without clothing! And he inflicted some crazy experiments on his children in the coldest weather! A woman, too, got this notion, and kept her infant

---

[86] Charles Codman, *A Brief History of the City of Modern Times, Long Island, N.Y. and a Glorification of some of its Saints* (Brentwood, NY, undated manuscript, approximately around 1905).

[87] Josiah Warren, *Practical Applications of the Elementary Principles of True Civilization to the Minute Details of Every Day Life: And the Facts and Conclusions of Forty Seven Years Study and Experiments in Reform Movements Through Communism to and in Elementary Principles Found in a Direction Exactly Opposite to and away from Communism, but Leading Directly to All the Harmonic Results Aimed at by Communism* (Princeton, Mass.: Published by the author, 1873) 17.

naked in the midst of winter!"[88] It is unclear how the rest of the community reacted to this episode as Warren failed to report whether other members of the Modern Times had taken any actions to deal with this eccentricity or perhaps even lunacy. There was a bit more involvement in a different case when "[a] German who was wholly or partly blind, paraded himself naked in the streets, with the theory that it would help his sight! He was stopped by an appeal to the over seer of the Insane Asylum. He could see well enough to take a neighbor's coat from a fence where the owner of it had been at work. This gave the neighbors an idea that we were a nest of thieves as well as fanatics".[89] Although clearly some measures were taken to isolate the perpetrator of this disturbance, there is no information who initiated this response and whether it was preceded by a discussion about the boundaries of the individual sovereignty of the aforementioned German. It seems unlikely that such an action had been taken by Warren himself or one of his followers as they remained strongly committed to the principles of individual rights. Yet, Warren also stated that: "To counteract this, hand bills were printed and circulated describing the person, and advising the neighbors who might miss any thing to come to that village and look for it in his premises. This placed the responsibility upon *him, Individually*, where it belonged, and put an end to his pilfering".[90]

Warren's attitude, combined with his convictions about the subjectivity of perception and the inadequacy of language to present universalities, led him not only to deny the possibility of adopting statutory law, but also to deny the existence of any other form of legal order. The very essence of a legal norm is that it has a general character – it applies to a group of individuals or to everyone and binds them without any exception. The norm, if it is not specified otherwise, binds the individual in any moment of their life in a situation that is specified in the legal norm. Even in the common law tradition one can find attempts to look for some generalisation and refer to the precedence, searching for some commonalities between previous and current cases. Warren's entire epistemological and ontological system is built upon withdrawing from generalisation and following particularity and contextualisation. Therefore, for Warren not only was the legal framework inadequate for individual cases and particular circumstances, but so was the common law judiciary system. He argued that "[l]aws cannot be adapted to the individuality of cases, and if they could, laws are language which is subject to different interpretations according to the individuals who are appointed to administer them, therefore, it is individuals rather than laws that govern. Every election illustrates this: we are told that our destinies depend on the election of this or that man to office! why? this shows that it is m e n not laws or principles that govern society. There is an individuality among judges and jurors as among

---

[88] Warren, *Practical Applications* (1873) 17-18.
[89] Warren, *Practical Applications* (1873) 18.
[90] Warren, *Practical Applications* (1873) 18.

all other persons; so that he whom one judge or jury would acquit, another would condemn: Judge Jeffreys acquired the popular epithet of 'bloody Jeffreys' from the remarkable number of persons condemned under his administration of the same laws which in other hands would have acquitted them; there is no security in laws, we must seek it elsewhere. Citizens cannot know today what will be lawful tomorrow; laws made this year are unmade the next and their repeal is often our only intimation that they existed. All these uncertainties must exist even when laws are framed with the greatest wisdom and administered with the purest devotedness to the public good without the least tinge of personal feeling or private interest, provided such phenomena are to be found, (...) laws and governments still are what they always have been viz. p u b l i c   m e a n s   u s e d   f o r   p r i v a t e   e n d s".[91]

The only actions that seemed appropriate and acceptable for Warren would be those in which any hypothetically generated costs (not limited to costs in an economic sense) would be covered completely by the person who performed those actions. Such a person would bear sole responsibility for his or her deeds and their possible consequences. Actions perceived as unacceptable were those when the cost was shared between the agent who made the decision and performed the action and the others. Warren condemned those addicted to alcohol, observing "[n]ow, we will take for instance the drunkard, he cannot act at his own cost because he involves his family in destruction and they must for self-preservation restrain him".[92] When we analyse Warren's premises and his philosophical framework we need also to consider an important question: is unlimited freedom possible? Initially unlimited freedom must be restricted by the self-preservation of others. Therefore, even Warren in his radicalism adopted an approach typical for many classical liberals, where the limits of liberty are drawn by the analogous sphere of the liberty of other individuals. The non-harm principle, even though not explicitly expressed, was rooted in the common human desire for happiness, something that was impossible to achieve in solitude. Desire for happiness forces one to look for the assistance of others in pursuing his or her own version of happiness and moderate his or her actions and mode of behaviour.

When we adopt Warren's premises it provokes another fundamental question, that is, whether the alcoholic addiction of a person who does not have a family and bears all the costs that his/her actions generate, taking sole responsibility, would be perceived as a violation in Warren's world of stateless order? Even if Warren did not accept the fact that such an addiction could be a source of happiness and keeping in mind that he strove to refrain from giving advice and imposing his vision of life, was it possible that based on the principle of individual sovereignty he would have accepted such actions, irrespective of his personal disapproval towards them? Then, Warren's approach seems to be quite close to the concept

---

[91] Warren, A brush 14.
[92] Warren, *Notebook D* 75.

that was later formulated by Lysander Spooner in his *Vices are not Crimes*,[93] and further developed by Murray Rothbard in *For a New Liberty*, where he coined the term "victimless crimes".[94] Warren's approach was based to some extent on something that might be called the economisation of axiology. Deeds would be acceptable as long as the agent was the only person taking the full consequences of his or her actions. The unlimited liberty and unlimited sovereignty of individuals was connected with their responsibility for themselves. To determine whether the action is justified and permissible it might be sufficient to determine who bear the consequences of action. Such mechanism allowed Warren to determine what kind of actions are acceptable without making any reference to the absolute, eternal, objectively existing concept of good or morality.

Warren offered an alternative to the traditional legal system, where the government, using its coercive power enacted and implemented the legal norms. Warren proposed that law should be dissociated from any governmental structures. The alternative would be provided by a system in which different bodies performed arbitrary and advisory services. "[A]ny person, of either sex, who may coincide with this proposition, and who feels competent to give Counsel in any department of human affairs, publicly announce the fact, as lawyers and physicians now do, or permit their names and functions to be made accessible to the public in some manner, so that whoever may need honest counsel on any subject may know where to find it. If a meeting of such Counsellors is thought desirable by any interested party, he or she can invite such as are thought to be most competent for the occasion, according to the subject to be considered. These Counsellors, while in session, would constitute a deliberative assembly, or advisory tribunal. It might consist of both sexes or either sex, according to the nature of the subject to be deliberated upon. After deliberation, or whenever any interested party feels ready to make up an opinion, let him or her write it down with the reasons for it, and present it to the Counsellors and the audience, for their signatures, and let the document go forth to the public or to the interested parties. If there are several such documents, those having the signatures of counsellors or persons most known to be reliable would have the most weight; but, in order to ensure any influence or benefit from either, let compensation come to the Counsellors like that to Rowland Hill, in voluntary contributions *after* the benefits of the opinions have, to some extent, been realized".[95] The system was thus to be financed on a completely voluntary basis by those who benefited from it.

Moreover, the system did not contain any form of penalty for any type of undesired actions (given Warren's ideas, it was hard to apply the term "prohibited" to such actions). Warren did not even consider the possibility that people could commit a serious crime, such as murder or rape. Advice and consultation would

---

[93] Spooner, *Vices*.
[94] Rothbard, *For a New Liberty*.
[95] Warren, *True Civilization* (1863) 28-29.

replace the legislative, executive and judiciary power. Warren asked rhetorically *"What will be the use of Congresses, Legislatures, and Courts of Law?"*[96] He also did not consider the usefulness of those institutions, as well as any compulsory isolation of criminals. The only form of penalty used would be social ostracism: "This absolute right of *Sovereignty* in every individual, over his or her *person, time, and property* is the only rule or principle known to this writer that is not subject to exceptions and failures as a regulator of human intercourse. It is very often, however, impossible, in our complicated entanglements, for one or some to exercise this right without violating the same right in others. We will ask our Counsellors to examine DISINTEGRATION as the remedy".[97] Therefore, disintegration and separation of interests, according to Warren, were a sufficient remedy to handle difficult situations and solve issues created by possible violations of absolute rights of others to make decision concerning personhood, property and time. Besides this sole existing norm – the absolute right to his or her person, property and time – there were no other legal norms.

When we adopt Warren's definition of law and how he defined the legal norm it poses the question whether it was a legal norm at all. There is no doubt that it has *sine qua non* character and *generalisation-abstraction* element definitely binds everybody and always. The most problematic, however, would be, the question of the sanction. Warren proposed mere expulsion and social ostracism, two relatively weak punishments (keeping in mind that even expulsion from the community, according to the records, was voluntary action taken by the violator as the result of earlier ostracism, and it was not supported by the use of coercion). When one takes into consideration the lack of use of coercive force (even in order to prevent violation of other people's rights) it seems quite surprising that Modern Times did not have more violent conflicts and that it lasted so long. But the evidence reveals also traces of Warren's more realistic views of human nature. Thus, in his 1857 account J.P David quoted Warren commenting his attempts to establish a community in the Midwest. Warren advised "that the fourth only of those who Promise can be relied on. I think it not safe to depend on so large a fraction. The reasons that these various persons have for this instability and non-performance of what they voluntarily propose, are best known to themselves".[98] This passage reveals Warren's bitter disappointment and possibly even pessimistic, vision of human nature.

Furthermore, when Warren's reports of his almost invariably successful experiments are compared against other primary sources his narrative begins to break down. Other authors writing about the Modern Times, the activities of which were well documented due to the community's proximity to NYC, presented a less optimistic vision of the cooperatives. Alfred Cridge noted that "Warren started with

---

[96] Warren, *True Civilization* (1863) 33.
[97] Warren, *True Civilization* (1863) 32.
[98] A letter from J P Davis 109.

the statement that 'An experiment in Social Science, organized by Josiah Warren and S. P. Andrews, is now being tried about 41 miles from New York, on the Long Island Railroad. Its principal bases are: Individual Sovereignty and Cost the Limit of Price. Its advocates oppose combination of interest under any circumstances, and thus may seem Anti-Socialist, but in reality, by withdrawing the elements of discord, they favor co-operation as far as a demand exists. Cooperation admits of individual control; combination does not; hence, discord, or a liability to it. Their principle, however sound, cannot be fairly tested in the locations they have chosen. The land is secured by Mr. Andrews to such as want it, at $28 per acre, which some people there think, much more than better land could have been bought for in the vicinity. It is good for fruit growing when cleared, provided manure enough is applied; but the scrub-oak with which the ground is covered, is extremely difficult to eradicate. Some say the land is leachy, and the musquitoes, not appreciating Warren's principles, do not adapt the supply to the demand. Two years since, about fourteen families were on the ground—not enough to carry out the principles. I presume they have not materially increased".[99] The remarks of Alfred Cridge reveal not only the sceptical attitude of the future participants of Warren's experiment. Cridge praised the individualistic, anti-socialist principles of Warren's philosophy, but the proximity of NYC, in his opinion, was a great disadvantage for two reasons: the land prices were too high and the number of the participants was insufficient to test Warren's principles in practise.

A significant crisis that Modern Times faced and that ultimately led to its dissolution was the arrival of Mary Gove Nichols and her husband, Thomas Nichols, the advocates for women's healthcare, water cure, vegetarianism and, what was more shocking, of free love doctrines. Their appearance led to increasing public association of Warren's experiments with promiscuity, the association that Warren tried to avoid. When the two conflicting visions about how the community should function emerged, Warren tried to fight with the Nicholses by arguing that they disseminated their opinion at the cost of others, destroying the good name of the members of the community. This action however, failed to solve the clash and exposed the weakness of Warren's system, demonstrating the inefficiency of the "cost principle" in preventing conflicts.

This conflict could have been predicted at the moment of the very foundation of the community. If one examines advertisements encouraging prospective members to join one can see that there were little, or no expectations toward them. Although they were informed that the settlement and the entire mode of life would be based on equity principles, there were no sigs that they were oblige to comply with the rules, as suggested. *Card to the Public* was signed by "citizens of 'Modern Times', Long Island, [located] two hours' ride from New York, upon

[99] Alfred Cridge, "Present position and future prospect of American socialism," *The Social Revolutionist; A Medium for the Free Discussion of General Principles and Practical Measures, Pertaining to Human Progress and General Well-Being* 1.1 (Jan. 1856): 10.

the Long Island Railroad". Anonymous authors stated: "We take this method of informing our fellow-citizens, who are desirous of bettering their condition in life by escaping from hostile competition, and obtaining and retaining for themselves the fall results of their own labor, that an opportunity is presented at this point, each as we believe exists where else. (...) We have been daring the past year residents here, and already experience great benefits from our location and the principles which have governed the settlement. We foresee far greater benefits with the increase of numbers. The object of the settlement is to furnish an opportunity to exchange labor equitably (bringing up the labor of women to the same prices as that of –men, etc.), (...) but no pledges are required, and no understanding, implied or expressed, is had with the settlers, that they are to live upon those principles or in any given way. They will be expected to do so just so far and no farther than they find their interest and their judgment impelling them to it. No conditions whatever are imposed except that the candidate for settlement shall receive an invitation to become a citizen after forming the acquaintance of parties on the ground, by letter or visit; in any way, in fine, by which they can be satisfied that he is a fitting person for such an enterprise. The spring is just now opening. (...) A broad and ample domain is secured, to be entered upon and possessed by laboring men and women who desire to achieve independence (...) This domain is offered to them, as no other lands upon which a town is to be built were ever offered; that is, without a dollar of profit or enhanced price above their prime cost, as wild lands".[100]

This passage highlights a peculiar situation: rather than introducing written constitution or a set of rules for the members, Warren's community offered them an invitation to act as they saw fit. This striking openness and unwillingness to set a structure for conduct explains future problems that inevitably arose. Some attempts to resolve these problems were made, as suggested by an article in *The Vanguards*. This, it appears, a pre-selection of members was introduced, leading to a more elitist membership model. The anonymous author reported that "several 'Equity' villages on Josiah Warren's plan, are in operation more or less successfully, in various parts of the Union; but it is not considered advisable at present to give the locations general publicity, as it is considered that by so doing, an unstable and unpractical class of dreamers (of whom the Nicholses may be considered types,) are attracted to them, and the success of such movements thereby considerably endangered".[101]

This passage indicates that Warren's solution was to open the community only to suitable candidates, true followers of his doctrine as it became clear that it was difficult to offer his vision to a broader audience. There was no effective mechanism of reconciliation with those who expressed a different opinion and did not adopt two most vital Warren's principles: sovereignty of individual and

---

[100] "Untitled," *Spiritual Telegraph* 23 Apr. 1853 (unpaginated).
[101] "Untitled," *The Vaneguards* 1.15 (June 1857): 115.

"cost the limit of price" principles. The experiment, thus, faced the conventional crisis, following the fate that has been shared by many who wanted to implement anarchism into practice. This crisis stemmed from their overly idealistic vision of human nature. As Codman wrote, "more than a handful of those who clamor for justice are honest and in earnest: those who prate and shout for it (...) are far from ready to practice".[102]

---

[102] Codman, *A Brief History* 25-26.

CHAPTER 2

THE WARRENITE ECONOMY

> When the first village of Equity was started, eight and a half years
> ago, the owner of the land bound himself by a written contract
> to sell to such persons as might be invited to settle there, at
> prices fixed then. This prevented speculation for three years. At
> the end of that time, another person bought about half of the
> unsold lots—paid money for them, and gave another bond to the
> citizens that they should be sold for cost
>
> *Josiah Warren, Periodical Letter, No. 3 (Boston)*, March, 1856, 42.

2.1. The *Time Store* experiment

The aim of this chapter is to show the major premises of Warren's economic
theory. What led Warren to controversially demand to make the cost of production
the final limit of the price? How such a demand could be fulfilled without
a violation of private property rights of the individual? What makes Warren
a unique thinker in his attempts to implement his theories and test the accuracy
of his premises. Therefore, the next task will be an analysis of the functionality
of Warren's economic experiments in practice. Consequently, to fully gain an
accurate perspective of the *Time Store* experiment, Warren's proposition needs
to be set in the broader context of Puritan economic traditions and various pre-
Ricardian economic theories. Warren seems to be the first author that was able to
reconcile the demand for liberty with the demand of equality (or equitability, as
Warren himself preferred the term *equitable*). That was possible because the entire
system was based on voluntarism, and those who decided to resign from surplus
income did it without any external pressure.[103] The last part presents the "fair
exchange" system promoted by Warren that he contrasted with the condemned
"social cannibalism".

---

[103] The only external pressures used in Warren's experiment were some forms of shaming and
social constrain, but they are rather soft measures compared with the systems based on obligatory
taxation.

2.1.1. The practical framework of the experiment

Josiah Warren opened his first *Time Store*, as he named his experimental shop, in Cincinnati on May 13th, 1827.[104] The *Time Store*, was also called the *Co-operative Magazine*. There is lack of precise information regarding when it ended, but according to Warren's own testimony, the experiment worked for almost three years – "during the whole three years I recollect but one person having withdrawn from co-operation".[105] The *Time Store* was the first scientific experiment in a cooperative economy in modern history.[106]

Although the *Time Store* operated for a relatively short time, Warren perceived it as highly successful and tried to re-establish it. His trip to New York in 1830 was partially undertaken to promote this idea. Despite his efforts, there was no interest in opening *Co-operative Magazine* stores that would work on Warren's principle.[107] Warren announced the opening of his *Time Store* in the local press; to popularise the idea he provided a detailed description of how the experiment would operate. Earlier articles had appeared in the *Western Tiller* in 1827 and 1828. Warren first had mentioned the idea of his *Co-operative Magazine* stores in September 1827; two more articles appeared in the *Mechanic's Free Press* on May 10th 1828 and on August 9th, 1828.

In the *Western Tiller* Warren explained that: "[a]t present many articles are purchase[d] with money – these are delivered out for the same amount of money which the keeper paid for them, and he is rewarded for his labor with an equal amount of the labor he receives from them, which is deducted from the note before mentioned. There are some articles, one part of which at present is procured with money, and the other has been deposited upon the new principle. That part of which money was paid, is paid for in money, and the other part is paid for in an equal amount of labor. We do not exchange labor for money, or money for labor, except in particular cases of necessity. The loss of any article after having been (*illegible*) is added to (*illegible*) part of its price. An account of all the *labor* and *money expenses* is kept, and when any one receives and article, he pays as much labor and money over and above the cost, as will likely to pay these expenses; the amount being liable to vary according to local and other circumstances, is

---

[104] Warren, To the Friends of Social System (21 Sept. 1827): 2.

[105] Josiah Warren, "Principles and progress of an experiment of rational social intercourse," *Peaceful Revolutionist* 1.2 (Feb. 1833): 7. Martin also noticed that when the shop stopped operating, it was "a controversial point among interested observers, Warren leaves no doubt about the matter". James J. Martin, *Men Against the State: The Expositors of Individualist Anarchism in America, 1827--1908* (Colorado Springs: Myles, 1970) 22. But Martin relied on Warren's report about the 3 years duration, and he referred already quoted here *Peaceful Revolutionist*, and also to *The Herald of Equity* 1 (Feb 1841): 6. and *The Herald of Equity* 1 (Feb 1841): 6.

[106] John Rogers Commons et al., eds., *A Documentary History of American Industrial Society*, vol. 5 (Cleveland, Ohio: The Arthur H. Clark Company, 1910) 78-79; Martin, *Men against*; University of Michigan, Labadie Collection, Agnes Inglis Papers, Box 32, Research and notes.

[107] W. Bryan, "Untitled letter," *British Co-operator* 1.7 (Oct. 1830): 160.

fixed periodically by the keeper. An open *record* is kept, upon which is noted in a simple and expeditious manner, *each article that is delivered:* and this is done by such method, that at meeting of those who are in the habit of dealing here, it can be readily ascertained how much *labor* and *money* have been received for the purpose of discharging there expenses: and if, when compared with the account of expenses, it appears that too much has been received, the overplus will be distributed equally unless any individuals choose to keep and account of the precise proportions of their dealing, in which case they will receive accordingly. If too little has been paid, all will see the propriety and necessity of supplying the deficiency, and therefore no *obligation* to that effect is required. The expenses are paid in this manner, in order to secure magazine against the chances of loss and to enable strangers to receive the benefits of establishment, without being under the necessity of returning at a future time for the purpose of discharging these little items of expense".[108]

Even at this early stage one essential element that contributed to the success of Warren's experiment was its total transparency and the participants' ability to monitor the spending and costs of transportation. Warren could not break off from the pecuniary relation, even though such intention appeared to be one of the main reasons behind the concept of entire experiment. Those articles that were purchased with money had also been sold for money. The next text in the *Wester Tiller* revealed the real motivation – Warren wanted to create a more equal social relationship among individuals, while at the same time trying not to encroach upon their individuality and individual rights.

Warren presented the opening transaction and the characteristics of his earliest customer: "The first articles that were delivered out were two small quantities of *Medicine, the* cost of which was 50 cents — but according to the common practice they would have cost one dollar. The purchaser was a female acquaintance whose income with her needle did not commonly exceed 25 cents per day. Therefore she saved, in this one instance, *two days' labour* in about ten minutes; for the keeper was employed about ten minutes, and received ten minutes of her needle-work in return for his service. Had she bought these articles in the common way, she would have given 24 hours of her labor for ten minutes of the keeper's, or *one hundred and forty-four times more than she received;* and yet the keeper would not have received that which was as intrinsically *valuable* as ten minutes of her needle-work".[109] This passage provides a thorough explanation about people's motivation to participate in such an exchange. The main incentive was the fact that the amount of goods received in the labour for labour exchange was considerably larger compared with the amount possible to acquire for the salary paid for the same time of labour.

---

[108] Warren, To the Friends of the Social system (14 Sept. 1827): 2.
[109] Warren, To the Friends of the Social System (21 Sept. 1827): 2.

In the first article published in the *Mechanic's Free Press*, Warren described the general ideas and rules behind the project. Publicising his success stories and describing to the editor the progress he had made, Warren wrote: "(...) I think you left before the cold weather commenced, and therefore have not witnessed the most important of our operations. As soon as the season became cool, there were great demands for cloths of various kinds, which I found no difficulty in procuring. I bought at the public sales on a credit of 60 and 90 days, and very often sold the goods in 6 days, and some in less time. The place now became crowded, although you know that it stands remote from the bustle of business; so much was this the case that I became so exhausted with buying and selling goods, and in talking and explaining that I was obliged to shut up the magazine, half of each day in order to rest from the fatigue and confusion occasioned by the business of the other half. But this produced so much disappointment to the country people & others, that I was induced to open again during the day-time. (...) One very important fact, that Messrs. Folger, Nye, Saunders, Pickering,[110] Burgen, Rider, and all those who were so much delighted at first, have not changed their views in the least, except by an increase of zeal in its favour; and many more who knew nothing of it nor had any correct views of the nature of justice between man and man, when you was here have become really enlightened on the all-important subject, and in their intercourse with others are now spreading the honest principle far and wide".[111]

In the subsequent passage, Warren described that "[t]he magazine has been enlarged to about double its former dimensions; the work was performed by seven Carpenters, all upon the time system, and by putting my labour against theirs, they have gained at the rates of from 1 to 50 dollars per hour. This would not be believed by any one who had not realized it by some experience, but you have seen something of its results. I have had Rice at 1 1/4 cents per pound, Codfish at 2 1/2 cents, while the standing prices are 6 1/2 and 8 cents for the former, and 8 for the latter. Medicines as usual.[112] Cloths at about 33 per cent. below the current prices; remarks will be rendered unnecessary by your own reflections upon these facts".[113]

There was also a greater flexibility among the participants of labour for labour exchange, and they had comprehensive skills, or were at least open to dedicating their time and efforts to acquiring such skills. As Warren stated: "[w]e have commenced shoemaking, and several have perceived the practicability

---

[110] It is worth noticing that in the end John Pickering became displeased with the labour for labour project, cf. John Pickering, *The Working Man's Political Economy: Founded Upon the Principle of Immutable Justice and the Inalienable Rights of Man; Designed for the Promotor of National Reform.* (Cincinnati: Stereotyped in Warren's new patent method by Thomas Varney, 1847).

[111] Josiah Warren, "Untitled letter to the editor, dated April 20th, 1828," *Mechanics' Free Press* 10 May 1828: 2, col. B; This letter is also quoted in Commons et al., *Documentary* 133-137.

[112] That is the wholesale price which varies from one to three hundred per cent. discount on standard retail prices. (Warren's original footnote).

[113] Warren, Untitled letter 2, col. B-C.

of learning a business which they never thought of before. Mr. Ashworth[114] made a pair of shoes at the first attempt, which none but a critic could perceive were not the production of an experienced workman; and many others have acquired a knowledge of this trade with equal facility. When we require instruction in any part with which we are not acquainted, we obtain it from some of our friends and pay them hour for hour in labour notes on the Magazine. I look upon these movements with great interest, for they are of immense importance to those who are now suffering by mystery and speculation".[115]

This passage shows not only the difficulties caused by the enormous interest generated by the *co-operative magazine*, but it also reveals the motivations of its participants. The major incentive was low prices, which in some cases were 2/3 lower than the regular price in other stores. The Warren's *Plan of the Cincinnati Labour for Labour Store* also demonstrates another important reason behind the store's popularity. Labour performed for exchange could be done by anyone after a short training as in case of a shoemaker. After a short time, the result of his labour would be as good as that of any trained and productive shoemaker. At this point, the passage also highlights the limitations of the system. In case of more complex production systems and articles that needed many and/or highly skilled workers, the system would not have functioned efficiently.

In the next publication entitled *Josiah Warren, Plan of the Cincinnati Labour for Labour Store*, also published in the Mechanic's Free Press, Warren offered an even more detailed description of how the *co-operative magazine* worked. The first part presented the "design and arrangements" and showed the ideological motivations behind the entire project. Warren attempted to demonstrate the universality of his economic proposition and to prove that the project could be appealing to anyone exhibiting common sense and sympathy.[116] He also tried to point out the malfunctions of the contemporary patterns of administrating property and correct them. Warren pointed out that "[w]hoever can for a moment, so far abstract his thoughts from his pecuniary concerns, as to look around him, and observe the evils, which the established laws and customs, with respect to the administration of property, are daily producing in what is called Civilized Society, must, if he is possessed of the least degree of sensibility, feel a strong desire, to remove these evils. That the inevitable tendency of these Laws and Customs, is to produce Ignorance, Want, and Wretchedness, to the majority of mankind, to the labouring and useful members of Society, we have only to refer to their condition, in those countries where the present arrangements have been longest in operation, and where a full and satisfactory trial of them has been made".[117]

---

[114] "Mr. A. is a gentleman of between 40 and 50 years of age, who had never before worked at any mechanical avocation". (Warren's original footnote).

[115] Josiah Warren, "Plan of the Cincinnati Labour for Labour Store," *Mechanics' Free Press* 9 Aug. 1828: 1, col. A.

[116] Warren seemed to be close in his premises to the Adam Smith's Theory of Moral Sentiments and the notion of sympathy as one of the leading factors shaping social relations.

[117] Warren, Plan of the Cincinnati: 1, col. A.

What Warren called "pecuniary relations" had enormous influence on social relations not only in the "Old World" but also in America. He expressed disapproval of the existing situation: "In these countries, abounding with everything that is desirable, we see the labouring and useful members of Society, who have produced every thing, starving in the streets for want; while some are rendered equally miserable from the anxieties of speculation and competition, and others for want of an object worthy of pursuit, are destroying their health, and shortening their lives by inactivity and apathy, or by luxuriously revelling upon the labour of the depressed. Insincerity among friends, Lawsuits between relations, Hypocrisy in religion – deception in trade – dishonesty, speculation and enmity between man and man, are only a few of the results of these laws and customs. Nor should we confine our observations to the old world only. Already have we in this country, made alarming progress in the road to national ruin; and unless some effort be made to prevent the accumulation of the wealth of the country, in the hands of a few, we instead of setting to the world an example of republican simplicity, of Peace and Liberty, shall soon add one more to the catalogue of nations, whom aristocracy has blasted, and whom inequality of wealth, has precipitated from a comparatively prosperous situation to the lowest grade of degradation and misery".[118]

Warren was aware that his experiment was conducted on a limited scale, but would "test the principles upon which it is based. And it will be a very easy and natural step, to make more complete and extensive arrangements whenever it may be desirable".[119] During his second stay in New Harmony, Warren prepared to open the second *Time Store* that operated in an analogous manner to the one in Cincinnati. The store was opened in New Harmony on March 22nd, 1842.[120] The medium of exchange was *labour for labour* notes and the value of goods and services was determined based on the time needed to perform the work. Later, Warren included into this value a previously completed training, which for the first time was considered a legitimate portion of the cost of labour. As in Cincinnati, "each individual decided the value of his own labor note, the expectation being that the general opinion of the people involved in the labor exchange would eventually set an average for the various products and services in terms of labor price".[121] The prices offered by Warren were much lower than those of his competitors and, as he stated, the shop was very popular not only among the inhabitants of New Harmony, but also in the neighbouring counties. According to J.W. Sweasey's report reprinted in *Equitable Commerce* in 1846, people travelled over 40 miles and, in Warren's owns testimony, for over 100 miles to exchange goods: "the store' was perfectly crowded with customers waiting to be supplied, some of whom

118 Warren, Plan of the Cincinnati: 1, col. A.
119 Warren, Plan of the Cincinnati: 1, col. A.
120 A. Butler, *Josiah Warren Peaceful Revolutionist*, dissertation, Ball State University 1978, UMI 7919881, 2; Warren, and Andrews, *Practical Details* (1852) 89-90.
121 Martin, *Men Against* 42-43.

were obliged to go away disappointed, after having waited, perhaps, two hours".[122] Ironically, the popularity of the store partially contributed to its failure. Other storekeepers in order to compete with Warren radically decreased their prices and, gradually, clients returned to their local stores instead of participating in the barter exchange.[123]

People could obtain more commodities for a smaller amount of money when they entered Warren's economic experiment. Also, the monetary reward for the labour of farmers and simple craftsmen in the traditional economic system was much lower than the gratification they received by labour notes in Warren's system. The only incentives for the upper classes was the satisfaction gained from participation in this honourable experiment. Warren announced that he was able to convince a few lawyers and doctors to participate in the labour exchange, probably to work *pro publico bono* and to refrained from collecting additional profits.

The shop closed down in March 1844.[124] Two years later, the idea behind the *Time Store* seemed to be appealing to local farmers, who campaigned in the local press for its reopening or the creation of a new one.[125] Disappointed by the apathy and lack of incentives among the members of New Harmony in the afterglow period, Warren travelled to Cincinnati in 1844 to give a series of public lectures and seek out more engaged supporters for his idea.[126] He proudly claimed the experiment was a success: "[w]hatever may be thought of the hopelessness or the unpopularity of reform movements, I will venture to assert that no institution, political, moral, nor religious, ever assumed a more sudden and extensive popularity than the *Time Store* of New Harmony".[127]

Primary sources regarding the *Time Store* are scarce; it is, therefore, difficult to verify the credibility of Warren's self-professed success. That said, from few available voice, we gain some critical insight into the history of this experiment. The first document is by John Pickering, who was mentioned by Warren in 1828 as a supporter of his ideas, but turned into a critic of the concept as labour for labour exchange two decades later. Pickering rejected the logic and probability of voluntary depravation of surplus income arguing:

"First. No one will sell house-lots for five dollars apiece, when he can just as easily get five thousand for the same.

Second. No one will sell coffee for ten cents a pound, when he can just as easily get sixteen for the same.

Third. No one will take one equivalent for an hour's service, when he can just as easily get from a hundred to a thousand for the same amount of service.

---

[122] Warren, and Andrews, *Practical Details* (1852) 90-91.
[123] Warren, and Andrews, *Practical Details* (1852) 92.
[124] Martin, *Men Against* 43.
[125] *Indiana Statesman*, February 1, 1845.
[126] Humphrey Noyes, op. cit., 97.
[127] Warren, and Andrews, *Practical Details* (1852) 91.

Fourth. No lawyer will take an equal amount of labor in exchange for his own services, when he could just as easily obtain five hundred times that amount! He would be an idiot if he did, and so would all the rest.

Now, is it possible that a sane individual would seriously make such a strange proposition to mankind? The proposition lies before me, in the book. But stranger still are the inducements held out to draw people into the adoption of these arrangements. (...) Where, then, is that great army of martyrs to come from, that can accomplish the result contemplated by Mr. Warren? The rich can never have a motive to embrace these arrangements; the poor may; but where is the necessary capital to come from? 'Labor notes' are not capital. Capital is labor already performed, and condensed into some permanent form".[128]

Another extremely critical example is a letter by James Penn Bennett, an inhabitant of New Harmony, who wrote to John Beale in North Yuba [CA]., in 1852: "[o]ur friend Josiah Warren, who has knocked his head against all the hard questions of the day until he is a little cracked, is a convert to the spirit knockings, has conversed with some of the notables of a by-gone-age, and may be they have become converts to this system or he would'nt believe in 'em. an strange anamoly![129] Mr. Hinkly is a believer also".[130] As this letter suggests, Warren appeared to some of his contemporaries as an obsessed prophet, preaching his theory of labour for labour exchange, and followed by his disciples who were motivated by faith in his gospel.

2.1.2. Warren's contribution to economic theory

There is no doubt that Warren's *Time Store* experiment was inspired by the works of Adam Smith and *An Inquiry into the Nature and Causes of the Wealth of Nations* in which Smith stated that labour can be the measurement of value: "Every man is rich or poor according to the degree in which he can afford to enjoy the necessaries, conveniences, and amusements of human life. But after the division of labour has once thoroughly taken place, it is but a very small part of these with which a man's own labour can supply him. The far greater part of them he must derive from the labour of other people, and he must be rich or poor according to the quantity of that labour which he can command, or which he can afford to purchase. The value of any commodity, therefore, to the person who possesses it, and who means not to use or consume it himself, but to exchange it for other commodities, is equal to the quantity of labour which it enables him to purchase or command. Labour, therefore, is the real measure of the exchangeable value

---

[128] Pickering, *The Working* 171-172.

[129] Original orthography, it should probably be *anomaly* and not *anamoly*.

[130] "Letter From James Penn Bennett, New Harmony to John Beale, North Yuba [CA]", 1852, April 31, New Harmony Correspondence 1812-1871, I series, Folder 71.

I would like to thank Franziska Bechtel for drawing my attention to this piece. Ich möchte mich bei Ihnen herzlichst bedanken.

of all commodities".[131] In addition to Smith, Robert Owen proved to be another thinker that impacted Warren's works. His earliest exposition of ideas might be found in *Essays on the Formation of Human Character*, published in New Lanark in 1812-1813.

Definitely inspired by Owen, and probably also by Smith, Warren started his *Time Store* experiment where, "BY THE NEW ARRANGEMENTS, *all Labour is valued by the Time employed in it.* Much might be said to show that, as Time is above all things most valuable, that Time is the real and natural standard of value. But we will not now undertake to prove, that, which (upon reflection) no one will undertake to deny. We will rather proceed to give the arrangements which have been made to carry this principle into effect".[132]

When Warren described "[p]resent arrangements of the magazine" he showed that the entire exchange was based on a "... single and simple principle, all exchanges of articles and personal services are made, so that he who employs five or ten hours of his time, in the service of another, receives five or ten hours labour of the other in return. The estimates of the time cost, of articles having been obtained from those whose business it is to produce them, are always exposed to view, so that it may be readily ascertained, at what rate any article will be given and received. He who deposits an article, which by our estimate costs ten hours labour, receives any other articles, which, together with the labour of the keeper in receiving and delivering them, costs ten hours, or, if the person making the deposit does not wish at that time, to draw out any article, he receives a Labour Note for the amount; with this note he will draw out articles, or obtain the labour of the keeper, whenever he may wish to do so".[133]

Warren was aware that such a system would not be self-sufficient. However, "[i]n cases where the labour does not admit of being deposited, the person who receives it, gives a labour note to the Magazine, by which the bearer can draw out any articles which the Magazine may contain, as persons of all professions will require those things which do admit of being deposited. At present many articles are bought with money – these are delivered out for the same amount of money which the keeper paid for them, and he is rewarded for his labour with an equal amount of the labour of him who receives them, which is deducted from the note before mentioned. There are some articles, one part of which at present is procured with money, and the other has been deposited upon the new principle. That part for which money was paid, is paid for in money, and the other part is paid for in an equal amount of labour. We do not exchange labour for money, or money for labour, excepting in particular cases of necessity. (...) The keeper exhibits the

---

[131] Adam Smith, *The Glasgow Edition of the Works and Correspondence of Adam Smith vol. 1-2 An Inquiry into the Nature and Causes of the Wealth of Nations: Vol. 1-2.* W. B. Todd (Ed) Oxford: Clarendon, 1975 47.

[132] Josiah Warren, "Plan of the Cincinnati Labour for Labour Store," *Mechanics' Free Press* 1.31 (Aug. 9, 1828): 1, col. A.

[133] Warren, Plan of the Cincinnati: 1 col. A.

bills of all his purchasers to public view so that the cost of every article may be known to all. There is a list upon which each individual who is in the practice of dealing here, can make known his wants, and the keeper of the Magazine reports each day the articles or labour that can be received, and those who wish for the employment, refer first to the report of their wants to know whether their articles or services are required-as none can be received which are not wanted. When the keeper has occasion for money, he reports upon the list of wants the rate at which he is willing to receive it in exchange for his labour. There is a place for advertisements, so that communications can be made to all interested. When any one wishes to deal in the common way, and feels no interests in the new arrangements, the keeper will deal in that way, provided the profits will amount to that which he requires in money as the reward of his labour for that day".[134]

At this stage, Warren's greatest achievement was to take Smith's concept and implement it literally into economic transactions among people. Such implementation resulted in an equal exchange of labour for labour. Moreover, Warren overcame the long-time dilemma of the clash of equality with private property. His ideal reconciled both. Warren was able to overcome the wage differences and inequalities among people, at the same time keeping the rights of the individual to their person and to the labour intact. There was little chance to completely and totally eradicate differences in the reward for labour, but Warren's project radically minimised them. Labour for labour exchange allowed to implement the equitist ideal and at the same time prevented the individual's rights from being encroached upon.

"When we examine the state of society in which we live, it is perceived that some individuals receive one cent per hour for their labor or services, and that others receive, sometimes, twenty thousand dollars per hour for their labor or services. (...) But in the *Time System* (as it is called) the labor, or services of every individual (male and female) is rewarded, EQUALLY, without any regard to their employments. In the *present system*, it is the common practice for each individual to get as much money for his labor, as he has the *power* to obtain In the *Equal Exchange System* TIME is considered the REAL standard of value, in the place of money: And till labor or service is valued by the Time employed in it. And an hour of the labor of one individual in given for an hour of any other individual's labor[135]".[136]

It should be noted that at the early stage of his economic experiment Warren proposed a simple exchange – hour for hour. In his publication from 1863, he explained why he had to modify his assumptions. "It soon appeared, however,

[134] Warren, Plan of the Cincinnati: 1 col. A.

[135] "An average, from the labour of adult workmen, is taken as a standard: and the labour cost of each article is ascertained and fixed by this standard. And if any individual produces slower or faster than an average workman in the different branches of labour, he or she receives accordingly" – Warren's footnote.

[136] Josiah Warren, "Time Store," *Western Tiller* 12 Sept. 1828: 20.

that the more pleasant pursuits would be overcrowded by competitors who would ruin each other, while the equally necessary professions were shunned, and a large portion of wants would be left unsupplied. For instance, a steam saw-mill was to be kept running night and day in the winter time. The night tour was a great deal more disagreeable or uncomfortable than the day tour. All hands preferred the day tour at the same price. It was arranged so that the compensation for ten hours at night would equal that for fourteen hours of the daytime. Here was one recognition of the element of repugnance or *cost* as the necessary adjusting power".[137]

Moreover, Warren disavowed silver – or gold—backed currency. He wanted to implement a medium that would be backed by labour, something that could be used as a measurement to compare all labour and effort. As a result, the system became more complex and, in order to evaluate the value of labour, the time principle remained the main factor, but the element of revulsion was added (it was quite a subjective element and different individuals would probably have felt different levels of repugnance at the same labour activities). Therefore, apart from time, Warren implemented corn as another measurement unit. He argued in 1846 that "If a shoemaker thinks his labor not so costly as the raising of corn, (as he can work all weathers and with less wear of clothing and tools,) by one – quarter, then he can give his note for ten hours labor in shoe-making, or *two hundred and twenty-five pounds of corn*, which is one quarter less for the same time".[138] He returned to the same subject a few decades later: "Some staple article of the particular locality, such as corn or wheat, is selected as a *Unit* by which to compare and measure all other labours, as we now measure them by dollars and cents. For instance, after ascertaining how many pounds of corn is the average product of an hour's labour, say it is ten pounds, then any labour, which the performer of it considers as *costly* as corn-raising, would be rated at ten pounds per hour. If only half as *costly*, only five pounds, etc".[139]

A related point to consider is the fact that the idea of using corn as a medium of exchange corresponded with Smith's concept that "Woollen or linen cloth are not the regulating commodities by which the real value of all other commodities must be finally measured and determined; corn is".[140] This inconsistency and fluctuation between labour and corn as a determinant of the appropriate value, was noticed by Ricardo, who, in the opening pages of his *Principle*, complained: "Adam Smith who so accurately defined the original source of exchangeable value and who was bound in consistency to maintain that all things became more or less valuable in

[137]   Warren, *True Civilization* (1863) 84.

[138]   Warren, *Equitable Commerce* (1846) 77.

[139]   Warren, *True Civilization* (1863) 84-85.

[140]   Adam Smith, *An Inquiry Into the Nature and Causes of the Wealth of Nations, Vol. I ed. R. H. Campbell and A. S. Skinner, vol. II of the Glasgow Edition of the Works and Correspondence of Adam Smith* (Indianapolis: Liberty Fund, 1981) 516. It also worth looking at Ricardo's "corn theory of profit" in this context.

proportion as more or less labour was bestowed on their production has himself created another standard of value (...) after most ably showing the insufficiency of a variable medium such as gold and silver, [he] has himself by fixing on corn or labour, chosen a medium no less variable".[141]

The most shocking economic proposition was to limit the prices of all commodities by their cost of production, while the participants of the exchange would voluntarily resign from any surplus profits. Such an avant-garde idea would also lead to the denial of the law of supply and demand, and abolishment of competition. Warren wanted to change the economic and social relations among participants of equitable commerce and labour for labour exchange by voluntarily waiving any surplus profit. Although the *Time Store* was based on this rule, Warren had not presented the entire idea to the public prior to the 1840s. In the *Gazette of Equitable Commerce* in 1842, Warren wrote that "the COST in money or labor should be the *limit of price*. For instance, that goods should be sold for the amount of money and labor which they are purchase and delivery *cost*".[142] He returned to this subject in his *Letter of Equitable Commerce* published in 1844, where he said that the main purpose of his equitable commerce enterprise would be to "disconnect **value** from the **cost**, and recognize ultimate **cost** only as the just basis and limit of price in all pecuniary commerce, in opposition to the common practice of making cost to the holder and v a l u e   t o   t h e   r e c e i v e r of those limits".[143]

As Renate Perskon observed, "In order to arrive at a just evaluation of the product of labor, it is necessary, according to Warren, to have a clear understanding that all conceptions of political economy concerning 'value' rest upon arbitrary and unjust assumptions. Value is an uncertain term which depends upon circumstances that are unpredictable and in a constant state of flux. The contractor who exploits the economic needs of the workers and robs them of a portion of their labor, the owner of a piece of land which he did not create and who leases it and retains the unearned rent, the money-lender who charges interest on a sum of money based on the need of the borrower, all live at the expense and on the labor of others without creating any social value themselves. By making the need for a product the key to its price, a system of exchange is perpetuated which subjects the masses of people to the economic control of a minority. Consequently, the free self-determination of one's individuality becomes impossible".[144]

Forgoing surplus income was also supposed to abolish competition and provide the harmonisation of all interests since the participants of the exchange,

---

[141] David Ricardo, *On the Principles of Political Economy and Taxation*, ed. P. Srafta, *The Works and Correspondence of David Ricardo*, vol. 1 (Cambridge: Cambridge University Press, 1981) 14.

[142] *Gazette of Equitable Commerce* 1.2 (September 1842).

[143] Josiah Warren, *Letter on Equitable Commerce* (New Harmony: J. Warren, 1844) 2.

[144] Renate Perkons, "Benjamin R. Tucker— a fighter against his age: An interpretation of the dominant spokesman for individualist anarchism in America, 1881-1908," unpublished MA thesis. UMI 1S36963, 32.

by making their needs known to the public, would avoid shortages of supplies or overproduction. In his published works from the 1860s, Warren was even more uncompromising, demanding that while "Costs being made the basis and limit of price, there would be no disturbing preference for one pursuit rather than another; the strife would be at an end—the supply (...) would be in proportion to the demand—no disturbing fluctuations in prices would ever occur—wars for the profits of trade would be at an end—the poorest would be abundantly rich—temptations to frauds and encroachments of all kinds would cease, and laws and governments for the 'protection of person and property' would be unnecessary, and their desolating career might be brought to a close! This simple justice (cost—the limit of price) (...) would irresistabl[y] abolish every form of slavery under the sun".[145]

Warren blamed the contemporary legal order for establishing and sustaining the system that allowed value to be determined by the law of supply and demand, something that he considered unjust and leading to social cannibalism. That is why he insisted: "Legislators! Framers of institutions! Leaders of the public mind! Behold your most fatal error! You have suffered Value instead of Cost to become the measure of price in all the business of the world! Hence the ruinous rate of competition (...) the principal cause of the wars of nations (...) Hence, also, the insecurity in all conditions of life, and the universal scramble for unlimited accumulations of property (...) as the highest attainable good! (...). The Origin of Rich and Poor!—The fatal pit-fall of the working classes!—The political blunder!—The hereditary taint of Barbarism!—The subtle and all-pervading poison of civilization"![146]

Warren's observation of human differences displayed his faith in the ideal of economic equality.[147] Assuming that different individuals contributed differing amount of energy and time into the accomplishment of various ends, he proposed the substitution of equal opportunities with access to land, raw materials and credit. His scheme rejected the idea of paying for natural resources that were not the product of human labour.[148] However, unlike later anarchists, Warren continued to think of land as an object fit for sale, which was a glaring inconsistency. That said, as for the other "spontaneous fruits of nature" (the raw materials derived from the land), he held that these were no more appropriate objects for monopoly and sale than sunshine or air. However, he clarified this point, stating that "though the property or wealth is common to all (natural wealth—land, water, other resources), there is no communism or joint ownership between any".[149]

Machinery, in Warren's view, was socially beneficial only as long as it made products available to consumers priced in terms of the cost of production.

---

[145] Warren, *True Civilization* (1863) 82.
[146] Warren, *True Civilization* (1863) 83.
[147] Warren, and Andrews, *Practical Details* (1852) 75.
[148] Warren, and Andrews, *Practical Details* (1852) 14.
[149] Warren, *True Civilization* (1863) 126.

Labourers displaced by machines could seek employment in other activities not yet fully mechanised while benefitting from cheaper products now resulting from technological innovations.[150]

The *Time Store* operated from 1828 untill 1830, but Warren rejuvenated the project in 1842, when he returned to New Harmony (Indiana) and opened the second *Time Store*. The positive results of the experiment suggested that Warren had created a coherent system that protected individuality, avoided coercion and ensured the implementation of the egalitarian ideal.

2.2. *Time Store* in a broader perspective – various non-monetary theories and practices

In the early 1800s economy, to a great extent, was based on barter exchange. To illustrate this, James Henretta recalls the example of Merriam brothers who "[e]very year between 1818 and 1831 (…) traded with 25 to 30 storekeepers in small settlements throughout southern New England (over the years, a total of 91 rural merchants in 26 towns), exchanging their own imprints goods to feed and clothe their families and apprentices; the remainder were "recycled" into the local exchange economy, balancing out accounts with local suppliers and artisans. (…) They paid their journeyman primarily in kind—the rent of a small house, credits to his accounts at local stores, and no less than one-third of his 'wages' in books, which he apparently had to peddle for himself if he wished for more than a literary 'profit' from his labors. The Merriams also 'sold' books at their office and took almost anything in return: rye, corn, veal, cheese, butter, pumpkins, onions, firewood, and lumber in goods; mercantile credits from shoemakers; and even a little cash, primarily from members of the professions: ministers, doctors, and lawyers".[151]

This complex and organic system started to collapse when the suppliers demanded payments in bank notes or other "negotiable instruments of a cash economy". This had serious consequences for the "Merriams [who] had never handled $200 in cash over the course of a year; now they had to come up annually with $800 to $1,500".[152] They were forced to abandon the traditional rural barter system and shifted to the money exchange market system instead.

As Murray Rothbard pointed out "The monetary system of the country was not highly developed (…) The currency of the United States was on a bimetallic standard, but at the legal ratio of fifteen-to-one gold was under-valued, and the bulk of the specie in circulation was silver. Silver coins were largely foreign,

---

[150] Warren, *Equitable Commerce* (1846) 11-12; 17; 40-41; 45.

[151] Henretta, The 'Market' 295-296. Henretta's arguments are solely based on Jack Larkin, *The Merriams of Brookfield: Printing in the Economy and Culture of Rural Massachusetts in the Early Nineteenth Century* (Worcester, Mass.: American Antiquarian Society, 1986).

[152] Henretta, The 'Market' 296.

particularly Spanish, augmented by coins minted in Great Britain, Portugal, and France".[153] To get an even more comprehensive and deeper understanding of the monetary situation of the early republic and its citizens' attitudes toward paper money, it is worth following the analysis provided by Henretta,[154] who in turn referred to the concept created by Karl Polanyi. Polanyi made a distinction between the commodity money and the token money. According to him, money as a commodity was mainly used for foreign trade and was "simply a commodity which happens to function as money, and its amount, therefore, cannot, in principle, be increased at all, except by diminishing the amount of the commodities not functioning as money. In practice commodity money is usually gold or silver, the amount of which can be increased, but not by much, within a short time".[155] The money that he called token money (paper money) was used only for domestic trade. As William Stanley Jevons correctly pointed out, "token coins (...) are defined in value by the fact that they can, by force of law or custom, be exchanged in a certain fixed ration for standard coins. The metal contained in a token coin has of course a certain value; but it may be less than the legal value in almost any degree".[156] However this "fixed ratio" was quite dynamic in the early republic.

Paul A. Gilje, observing and analysing the early development of the banking sector in the 1780s and 1790s, pointed out that "[b]anks as institutions were marvelous (and I do not mean this term in a necessarily positive manner) tools for creating capital. They literally pulled money out of thin air. (...) Each of these institutions printed its own notes, creating a patchwork currency that boggles the mind in terms of size, color, and design. Although this lack of consistency proved confusing (and a boon to counterfeiters) it worked wonders during the early republic by providing both a means of exchange, and increasing levels of capital for investment. These banks printed more currency than their net worth and cash reserves. (...). Of course there were times when these inflationary bubbles would burst, but inevitably the cycle would start up again, driven, in part by the creative energies of bankers".[157]

Being aware that unlimited print of money by the banks might have an inflationary effect,[158] a prohibition of state-issued token money was included into

---

[153] Rothbard, *The Panic* 1-2.

[154] Henretta, The 'Market' 296-297.

[155] Karl Polanyi, *The Great Transformation: The Political and Economic Origins of our Time* (Boston, Mass.: Beacon Press, 2010) 202-203.

[156] W. S. Jevons, *Money and the Mechanism of Exchange* (New York: D. Appleton, 1875) 74.

[157] Paul A. Gilje, "The Rise of Capitalism in the Early Republic," *Journal of the Early Republic* 16.2 Special Issue on Capitalism in the Early Republic (Summer, 1996): 163-164.

[158] There is vast literature about the early stage of the discussion related to paper money, especially in the context of the First Bank of America, the Federalist vision of the currency policy. See. Janet A. Riesman, "Money, Credit, and Federalist Political Economy," *Beyond Confederation: Origins of the Constitution and American National Identity*, ed. Beeman, R. R., Botein, S., Carter, E. C., & Institute of Early American History and Culture (Williamsburg, Va.) (Chapel Hill: Published

the federal constitution. Therefore, state could not issue "coin money, emit bills of credit; make anything but gold and silver a tender in payment of debts; pass any (...) law impairing the obligation of contracts".[159]

It is essential to keep in mind the strong impact this shift from traditional rural barter system toward money exchange market system might have had on the inhabitants of New England at the time of the Panic of 1819.[160] The sources are silent about the motives behind Warren's decision to migrate from Boston to the Midwest in 1819, but it is hard to overlook the economic factors that may have influenced his decision; namely the frontier offered more opportunities. In the light of this, it is most likely that his personal observation of the impact the Panic of 1819 had on ordinary people strengthened the conviction that token money was not a reliable guarantee of value.

William Beck, in his early work *Money and Banking, Or Their Nature and Effects* from 1839, refers to this concept. "Real payment in all exchanges, is labor for labor, or what is the same thing, the obtaining of the production or commodity, which, a man requires for his own use, in exchange for that surplus portion of his own, which, in the prosecution of his professional industry, he has produced for the service of the community. Commodity is what every one wants. Commodity is what he must consume. When he exchanges the productions of his industry for the commodity he wants, he makes a real exchange, when he sells them for money, he makes but half the exchange, the other half is effected when he exchanges that money for commodity and in proportion to his cunning he delivers or he receives a surplus value without or beyond an equivalent".[161]

The idea of paper money representing a certain amount of labour rather than a certain precious commodity was held in common and developed separately by several radical economic thinkers in the first half of the nineteenth century as well.[162] In the early 1820s, besides Owen's early writing, similar concepts, albeit

for the Institute of Early American History and Culture, Williamsburg, Virginia, by the University of North Carolina Press, 1987) 128-161. Janet A. Reisman, "Republican Revisions: Political Economy in New York after the Panic of 1819," *New York and the Rise of American Capitalism*, ed. William Pencak and Conrad Edick Wright (Albany, NY: New York Historical Society, 1989) 1-44; Ronald Hoffman ed. *The Economy of Early America: The Revolutionary Period, 1763-1790* (Charlottesville: University Press of Virginia, 1988); Drew R. McCoy, *The Elusive Republic: Political Economy in Jeffersonian America* (Chapel Hill: University of North Carolina Press, 1980); Paul Gilje, "The Rise of Capitalism in the Early Republic," *Journal of the Early Republic* 16.2 (1996): 159-181.

[159] U.S. Constitution, art. I, sec. 10.

[160] Daniel S. Dupre, "The panic of 1819 and the political economy of sectionalism;" *The Economy of Early America: Historical Perspectives & New Directions*, ed. Cathy D. Matson (University Park, Pa: Pennsylvania State University Press, 2006) 263-293.

[161] William Beck, *Money and Banking, Or Their Nature and Effects Considered* (Cincinnati: William Beck, 1839) 42-43.

[162] Martin, *Men Against* 11-12; Noel W. Thompson, *The People's Science: The Popular Political Economy of Exploitation and Crisis, 1816-34* (Cambridge: Cambridge University Press., 1984); Noel W. Thompson, *The Market and its Critics: Socialist Political Economy in Nineteenth Century Britain* (London: Routledge, 1988); E. P. Thompson, *The Making of the English Working Class* (New York:

on a different scale can be found in the writings of John Gray's such as *A Lecture on Human Happiness*[163] and *The Social System*, where he perceived "labor as the only source of wealth".[164] Later, he made labour a standard by which the value of a commodity was to be estimated by the demand that "A producer we will here define to be a man, who, by the labour of his own hands, assists in the production of some consumable product, which may be either used or exchanged, after his labour is completed, for some other commodity which has cost an e q u a l q u a n t i t y   o f   l a b o u r".[165]

Another representative of the pre-Marxist socialists, William Thompson, in *An Inquiry into the Principles of the Distribution of Wealth Most Conducive to Human Happiness* determined the value of goods by the labour they embodied, combined with what was perceived as the social worth or social utilities of such goods.[166] In addition, John Francis Bray in *Labour's Wrongs and Labour's Remedy; or, the Age of Might and the Age of Right* from 1839 wrote that "It is labour alone which bestows value ; for labour, as it has been truly said, is the purchase money

Pantheon Books, 1964); Cathy D. Matson, *The Economy of Early America: Historical Perspectives & New Directions* (University Park, Pa: Pennsylvania State University Press 2006); Henry W. Spiegel, *The Growth of Economic Thought* (Englewood Cliffs, N.J: Prentice-Hall, 1971) 443-445; Janet Kimball, *The Economic Doctrines of John Gray 1799-1883* (Washington: Catholic Univ. of America Press, 1948); Gregory Claeys, *Owenite Socialism: Pamphlets and Correspondence* (London: Routledge, 2005) (introduction 1-20); Alfredo Saad-Filho, "Labor, Money, and 'labour-Money': a Review of Marx's Critique of John Gray's Monetary Analysis," *History of Political Economy* 25.1 (1993): 65--84; Esther Lowenthal, *The Ricardian Socialists* (New York: Columbia University, 1911); J. E. King, "Utopian or Scientific? a Reconsideration of the Ricardian Socialists," *History of Political Economy* 15.3 (1983): 345-373; Marianne A. Ferber, and Julie A. Nelson, *Beyond Economic Man: Feminist Theory and Economics* (Chicago: University of Chicago Press, 1993); Carol A. Kolmerten, *Women in Utopia: The Ideology of Gender in the American Owenite Communities* (Syracuse, N.Y: Syracuse University Press, 1998); Thomas E. Skidmore, *The Rights of Man to Property!: Being a Proposition to Make it Equal among the Adults of the Present Generation, and to Provide for its Equal Transmission to Every Individual of Each Succeeding Generation on Arriving at the Age of Maturity: Addressed to the Citizens of the State of New-York, Particularly, and to the People of other States and Nations, Generally* (New-York: Printed for the author by A. Ming, Jr., 1829).

[163] John Gray & London Co-operative Society, *A lecture on Human Happiness: Being the First of a Series of Lectures on that Subject, in which will be Comprehended a General Review of the Causes of the Existing Evils of Society, and a Development of Means by which they may be Permanently and Effectually Removed* (London: Sherwood, Jones, & Co., 1825).

[164] John Gray, *The Social System: A Treatise on the Principle of Exchange* (Edinburgh: W. Tait., 1831) 40.

[165] Gray, *The Social System* 242. Emphasis added.

[166] William Thompson, *An Inquiry into the Principles of the Distribution of Wealth most Conducive to Human Happiness: Appllied to the Newly Proposed System of Voluntary Equality of Wealth* (London: Printed for Longman, Hurst, Rees, Orme, Brown and Green, 1824) 1-17. Thompson is aware that even in cases when the law of supply and demand works, and we have what he called "objects of desire", even then "Labor is the *sole* measure of the value of an article of wealth, it does not assert that this sole measure is and all cases and *accurate* measure. As an article must be an object of desire to be an article of wealth, and so these desire and preferences are apt to vary with circumstances (...) Under representative self-government, they would be equally disregarded as things conferring merit, and reduced to their commercial value, to the value of real use". W. Thompson, *An inquiry* 15.

which is paid for everything we eat, or drink, or wear. Every man has an undoubted right to all that his honest labour can procure him. When he thus appropriates the fruits of his labour, he commits no injustice upon any other human being; for he interferes with no other man's right of doing the same with the produce of his labour".[167] As Noel Thompson wrote, "[t]hese writers did not attempt to expand such statements into a value theory of any degree of sophistication but it would be fair to interpret them as believing that commodities should exchange according to the labour time embodied in their manufacture and would do if the natural laws of value prevailed".[168]

Moreover, Robert Owen in his *Report to the county of Lanark* referred to labour as the measure of real value of a commodity.[169] While acknowledging Owen's influence, it is necessary to make a distinction between his writings and the impact of the English Owenite movement. As Edward Palmer noticed, "*Owenism* from the late Twenties onwards, was a very different thing from the writings and proclamations of Robert Owen. It was the very imprecision of his theories, which offered, none the less, an image of an alternative system of society, and which made them adaptable to different groups of working people. From the writings of the Owenites, artisans, weavers and skilled workers selected those parts which most closely related to their own predicament and modified them through discussion and practice".[170]

Similar theories of monetary substitutions were developed outside of England by Johann Karl Rodbertus in Germany and Pierre Joseph Proudhon in France.[171] However, as Martin observed, "[t]he simplicity of application of this idea by Warren is unique during a time confined almost entirely to theorizing about this

---

[167] John Francis Bray, *Labour's Wrongs and Labour's Remedy, or, The Age of Might and the Age of Right* (Leeds: D. Green, 1839) 33.

[168] N. W. Thompson, *The people's science* 91. This remark is accurate in reference to Thomas Hodgskin and John Francis Bray. In the passages that followed, Thompson admitted that John Gray and William Thompson are more difficult to label. However, analyzing the early writings of Gray and Thompson, I still find this analysis applicable to their theories.

[169] Robert Owen, *Report to the County of Lanark, of a Plan for Relieving Public Distress: And Removing Discontent, by Giving Permanent, Productive Employment, to the Poor and Working Classes, under Arrangements which will Essentially Improve their Character, and Ameliorate Their Condition, Diminish the Expenses of Production and Consumption, and Create Markets Co-extensive with Production* (Glasgow: Printed at the University Press, for Wardlaw & Cunninghame, 1821).

[170] E. P. Thompson, *The Making of the English Working Class* (New York: Pantheon Books, 1964) 789.

[171] Johann Karl Rodbertus, "Die Forderungen der arbeitenden Klassen," *Zur Beleuchtung der Sozialen Frage*, vol. 2, (Berlin: Puttkammer & Muehlbrecht, 1885) 195-223; Johann Karl Rodbertus, *Zur Erkenntnis unserer staatswirthschaftlichen Zustände* (Neubrandenburg: G. Barnewitz, 1842); Edward C. K. Conner, *The Social Philosophy of Rodbertus* (London: Macmillan 1899); Pierre Joseph Proudhon, *Qu'est-ce que c'est que la propriété, ou, Recherches sur le principe du droit et du gouvernement.* (Paris: Prévot, 1841); Pierre Joseph Proudhon, *System of Economical Contradictions; Or, the Philosophy of Misery.* Transl. Benjamin R. Tucker (Boston: B.R. Tucker, 1888); Dennis W. Brogan, *Proudhon* (London: Hamish Hamilton, 1934); Henry Cohen, *Proudhon's Solution of the Social Problem* (New York: Vanguard Press, 1927).

matter".[172] Among all those theoreticians, Warren was a bold and courageous practitioner who was the first to decide to test the practical applicability of the theory of value based on labour.

At the same time those ideas were widely disseminated in America, resonating within the debate about the proper reward for labour within a young industrial society, and about the ways of determining the just value of those commodities and labour. Thus, while Warren was first to practice the labour for labour exchange, he was not alone in this project.[173] In 1828 in Philadelphia, a Labour for Labour Association was formed. According to its constitution, any person (irrespective of sex) who was above 12 could be a member. "All articles that are entirely the produce of the labour of members of the association, or, for no part of which money has been paid, shall be valued by the number of hours, or parts of an hour, required for the production, and where different persons of the same profession, disagree in their estimates, the average of the whole shall be the price. A medium adult workman shall be taken as a criterion, but if females or children, perform the work, it does not in our opinion diminish its value. (...) All articles that are manufactured out of materials which cost money, shall be received at the store at the prime money cost of such materials, and the number of hours, or parts of an hour, required for their manufacture. (...) Any member depositing any article in the store, for the whole of which he paid money, will be required to present the bill of sale thereof to the committee of exchange, who will take a copy thereof, which, together with a list of the money cost, and labour value, of all articles received at the store, shall at all times be open to the inspection of all the members".[174]

Warren's attempts to establish a *Co-operative Magazine* in 1830 were futile. His second *Time Store*, which opened in New Harmony had a short life. However, in the late 1840s, the concept of labour for labour exchange became reinvigorated as Warren had further popularised it through the publication of *Equitable Commerce* in 1846 and its second edition in 1849, and a series of lectures delivered in New England. He issued labour notes that were used in Modern Times in the late 1850s.[175] In 1859 in Boston, a Dual Commerce Association was established; its members did not refer directly to Warren in their publication, but it is obvious that his philosophy of equitable exchange was an inspiration to them: "We use the

---

[172] Martin, *Men Against* 11-12.

[173] However, Commons made an excellent point observing that earlier in 1818 in Pittsburgh "The mechanics and manufacturers (...) organised the Pittsburgh and Vicinity Manufacturing Association to market their wares collectively (...) The scarcity of money and inadequate banking facilites made it necessary (...) to accept from country retail merchants 'other articles'". Consequently, they resorted to barter exchange, but there was no additional labor for labor principle measured by the time of dedicated labor. John R. Commons et al., *History of Labour in the United States* (New York: Macmillan, 1921) 95.

[174] First, published in *Mechanics' Free Press* 24 May 1828: 2, col. 2, 3. Reprinted in Commons et al., *Documentary* 129-133.

[175] Roger Wunderlich, *Low Living and High Thinking at Modern Times, New York* (Syracuse, N.Y: Syracuse University Press, 1992) 46-47.

word *association* for convenience, but in an exact sense. Not as an organization, but simply as a number of individuals actuated by similar motives voluntarily co-operating for the same great object, but carefully preserving the strict INDIVIDUALITY *of property and responsibility* as an indispensable element of order and success".[176] This passage evidently echoes Warren's own writings.

2.3. Voluntarism

When we consider enthusiasm for individualisation combined with the concept of sovereignty of each individual, the only possible option for Warren was to base all social and economic relations on absolute voluntarism. It provides the security of individual rights while at the same time creating a possibility of co-operation. "But LIBERTY is the vital principle of human happiness; and human nature seeks its *liberty* as the magnet seeks the north, or as water seeks its level; and society can never know peace until its members know LIBERTY; but it can never be realized under any organization of society now known to us, nor can it ever be attained upon any of the theories upon which societies are now acting! Whether any true theory is ever to be put in practice—whether justice is ever to take up its abode among us—whether LIBERTY is ever to be understood and enjoyed, are questions which yet remain to be determined in the uncertain future".[177]

In his *Notebook*, in the passage entitled "voluntary subordination", Warren wrote that "Natural liberty or Individual Sovereignty calls for freedom of choice in all cases under all circumstances & at all times. By freedom of choice I mean exemption from the control of other persons in distinction from the natural and irrestible control of circumstances. All social arrangements should admit of this freedom of choice of every individual and all subordination should be voluntary".[178] Such lack of control does not exclude the possibility of submission or subordination, while "Natural liberty or individual sovereignty calls for freedom of choice in all cases, under all circumstances, and at all times. By freedom of choice I mean exemption from the control of other persons in distinction from the natural and irresistible control of circumstances. All social arrangements should admit of this freedom of choice of every individual and all subordination should be voluntary. For instance, in the performance of a piece of music at a private party each one who takes a part subordinates himself voluntarily to the lead of one person".[179] Being a musician, Warren quite often used this example writing a few decades earlier that "No subordination can be more perfect than that of an Orchestra; but it is all *voluntary*".[180]

---

[176] Dual Commerce Association. *The Dual Commerce Association: Its Experience, Results, Plans & Prospectus: First Report* (Boston, Mass.: Dual Commerce Association, 1859) 5.
[177] Warren, and Andrews, *Practical Details* (1852) 12.
[178] Warren, *Notebook D* 107.
[179] Warren, *Notebook D* 107.
[180] Warren, *True Civilization* (1863)18.

Such Warren's approach poses many questions. The first one concerns his implicit assumption about people's rationality. For Warren, every participant of his experiment, including a child, was an agent. Voluntarism was possible because people were not only rational in making decisions regarding their lives, but also responsible enough to accept the negative consequences of their actions. Moreover, Warren applied the same standard to children, including his own children, when he established voluntary agreements about modes of behaviour.[181]

When we look at Warren's report about the communities he established in the 1830s, it is clear how the principle of voluntarism guided the life of the participants. They adopted *Extracts From Minutes Of A Compact Association, Without Combination; Or, A Society In Which The Natural Liberty Of The Individual Was Not Violated*, the name alone suggesting that the society was based on individualism, bringing people together just to realise their individual aims, and not to pursue any form of common good. In response to the proposal to provide *Rules and Regulations for the government of the Society* in a written form, one of the members, E.C., "advocated simple *Liberty* ; that he did not wish to prevent others from trying any organization they might choose; that they ought *to be at liberty to bind themselves to act against their inclination whenever **it** might please them to do so*, but, for himself, he should act individually. He should decline entering into any bonds, or pledges, or organization, or combined responsibilities of any kind whatever. That he was ready to do whatever might, in his opinion, be within his power for the promotion of knowledge, but that he must be permitted to act solely from the interest which he might feel in *each individual action*, and must be FREE to judge, in each individual case, how far he could act with, or like others, and how far to differ from them".[182]

Declining to enter into any bonds, or pledges, or organization is evidence that Warren himself, and his disciples, were hostile toward any form of artificial constraint and binding. When the testimony of E.C. was welcomed with a vibrant discussion, it was "taken by E. C. as proof of the necessity of preserving the *liberty* to differ, and as proof that any demand for conformity could produce nothing but confusion".[183] Later attempts undertaken to organise the activities more formally were rejected after facing strong, serious protests. All members believed that "no association can attain any objects by an organization which destroys the liberty of its members, and that all objects aimed at by organizations can be attained without them. It was said by a *lawyer*, in reply, that there was *no precedent* for any such mode—that a society in which every one was perfectly at liberty, was no society

---

[181] I am highly indebted to professor Mika Lavaque Manty for pointing my attention to the problem of children and authority in the context of Warren's philosophy. Cf. H. Graham, "Political Theory and the Child: Problems of the Individualist Tradition," *Political Studies* 27.3 (1979): 405--420.

[182] Warren, and Andrews, *Practical Details* (1852) 50.

[183] Warren, and Andrews, *Practical Details* (1852) 51.

at all—it was a contradiction of terms".[184] The first four meetings focused only on providing a forum for expressing opinions. The majority made propositions that were always contested by the members of the minority. Throughout this entire process of discussion, members of the community paid great attention to the idea of individual freedom. Their major consideration was to guarantee that none of the adopted changes failed to allow *"assuming control over persons* and carrying measures by votes of majorities, or *the right of the strongest* (...) They also endeavored to show means by which, in this small way, people could associate together and attain certain purposes, as a body, *without* violating this freedom of person; and this minority, without waiting for the concurrence of the majority, went straightforward, without obstacle or difficulty, in the meetings, which, from that time, have *always without* exception been harmonious, orderly, and beneficial".[185] According to Warren, due to the intervention of the members of the minority, they "left any one FREE to act according to his own views".[186] During the entire process they did nothing that would encroach on individual liberty and the members were able to act based on voluntarily taken actions.

A major limitation of this report is the lack of information revealing what the members agreed upon and what they decided to do with those who displayed insubordination to the rules established by Warren. Was there any possibility to use force to remove from the community those who did not want to participate in a discussion which was perceived as a long and ongoing process of reaching consensus? Warren did not provide direct answers, but knowing that social ostracism was the only measure taken to restore order within the community, it is clear that Warren had high hopes and expectations for human behaviour and human nature itself.

Once again, unlimited liberty did not exclude cooperation as long as it was voluntary while "[i]t is between the control or force of circumstances or necessity each being his own judge of it and the control or force of persons or authority that we must draw the great broad line which is to distinguish voluntary from involuntary subordination. The one is in perfect accordance with a natural personal liberty which constitutes the chief element of the happiness of human beings and the other violates it and is the chief cause of the Bedlam like confusion which pervades all".[187]

When making decisions (regarding political, social or economic arrangements), individuals verbally expressed their consent on a voluntary basis. They could join the enterprise based on carefully established principles and were free to withdraw from it at any time. Warren condemned all other non-voluntary arrangements. "It is worse than useless, it is calamitous, to legislate as if it were possible to divest

---

[184] Warren, and Andrews, *Practical Details* (1852) 52.
[185] Warren, and Andrews, *Practical Details* (1852) 53.
[186] Warren, and Andrews, *Practical Details* (1852) 54.
[187] Warren, *Notebook D* 107.

ourselves of this involuntary instinct of self-preservation or self-sovereignty, and those who accept or act *on* such pledge commit as great an error as those who give it, and all contracts to this effect being impossible of fulfilment are null and void. We may delegate the *leading* function often with advantage, but it is folly, blindness, self-deception, and may be ruin, to commit ourselves *unqualifiedly to implicit and unhesitating obedience to any personal lead for a single hour*".[188] The entire social aspect of living in this manner is based on a highly individualistic vision of social order. Moreover, the social aspect is limited to the "interchange of ideas and cultivation of the social sympathies, by meetings—by the Press, by Conversations, readings, short addresses, remarks, recitations songs choruses, Instrumental music dancing and other social amusements".[189]

The co-operation was supposed not only to be voluntary, but also, have a specified time-frame – necessary to achieve a particular goal. After adopting such ideas of cooperating just for a short time and being purpose oriented, it was hard to find in Warren's philosophy any premises inducing individuals to continue cooperation before defining the next goal. There was no temptation to leave the natural state of unlimited liberty and individual sovereignty. The temporal and ad hoc need for voluntary co-operation could not be sufficient incentive to abandon this semi-state of nature.

Warren presented several case studies to contextualise his theory, demonstrating practical applications of voluntarism. One of them was the process of house building: "A man wants to raise a house; he cannot do it alone, and invites his neighbors to help him. They are willing to do so, either from sympathy, for the enjoyment of the companionship of the occasion, or for pecuniary compensation, or without any particular conscious motive. Whether they are moved by one motive or another, their movement is voluntary, and the raising of the house is the *point of coincidence* between them— the object which brings them together, and which gives rise to the co-operation between them".[190]

As Butler pointed out, "[l]ong before Kropotkin's theories of mutual aid, Warren stressed voluntary cooperation between individuals. This voluntary cooperation extended only as far as the labour of the individual and the aid given through respect for the individual; he retained property rights".[191] Commons presented Warren's voluntarism in a broader context – as one of many stages in the development of voluntary cooperation. "In the same way, the ideals and methods of voluntary cooperation have changed, according to circumstances and philosophies, from the distributive co-operation of all classes of consumers, the anarchistic co-operation of Josiah Warren in the thirties, and the communistic co-operation of Fourier and the 'associationists' in the forties, all of them based on

---

[188] Warren, *True Civilization* (1863) 131.
[189] Warren, *Notebook D* 117.
[190] Warren, *True Civilization* (1863) 127.
[191] A. Butler, Notebook D, *Introduction* ii.

a philosophy of harmony of interests of all classes, to the 'substitute for strikes' of the trade unionists of the sixties and the cooperative commonwealth of the Knights of Labour in the seventies and eighties, based on a philosophy of antagonism of interests".[192] In this view, it was essential that this anarchist cooperation remained the one that upheld individual sovereignty and individual rights without any coercive interference of any external (governmental or social) forces.

2.4. Fair exchange versus social cannibalism – combining equality and liberty

The principle established by Warren stated firmly that the cost of the production set the limits of the price. Warren refused to accept any profit that was not intended to cover the cost of production. This principle was formulated in the most extreme way; also today, advocating for forgoing any additional profit seems to be a form of utopian preaching. However, when this idea is placed in a broader context, it looks like just another voice in the old discussion. On the one hand, it was deeply rooted in the American Puritan religious tradition, or looking even deeper, embedded into Christian mediaeval ethics. On the other hand, it corresponded with the Lockean concept of property, where the right to property was established as the result of improvement – therefore labour value was added to things that were in a state of nature.

Since the twelve century, various European theologians and philosophers within the Judeo-Christian tradition had discussed the notion of just price. Thomas Aquinas asked in the second part of his *Summa Theologica* "[w]hether it is lawful to sell a thing for more than it's worth". The prominent voice in the discussion was that of the members of the School of Salamanca, among them Domingo de Soto, who in his treaties *De justitia et jure* asked whether merchants should freely set the price, based solely on their judgment. A Christian answer given to this question by Aquinas that "[i]t is altogether sinful to have recourse to deceit in order to sell a thing for more than its just price"[193] shows the real context of this discussion. We will see that the question of just price was perceived in an ethical and moral context rather than being limited to a purely economic consideration. Discussions about the proper price were a part of a larger debate on the nature of justice and just relations in society.

In Warren's case, it is even more appropriate to look at the Puritan heritage. "Calvin and his disciples placed work at the center of their social theology (...) All work in this society is invested with divine approval. Any social philosopher or economist exposed to Calvinism will be tempted to give labor an exalted position in his social or economic treatise, and no better way of extolling labor can be

---

[192] Commons et al. *History of Labour* 18.
[193] Summa Theologiae, II^a – IIae q. 77 a. 1.

found than by combining work with value theory, traditionally the very basis of an economic system. Thus value becomes labor value, which is not merely a scientific device for measuring exchange rates but also the spiritual tie combining Divine Will with economic everyday life".[194]

One of the earliest attempts to establish the moral standards of just price was the case of Robert Keane. As John Winthrop reported in his *Journals*,[195] Keane was accused of overcharging customers and sentenced by court to pay a two hundreds pound fine. The case also prompted John Cotton to remind in his sermon that "A man may not sell above the current price".[196] All those voices tried to show that instead of pure laws of demand and supply there was, and there should be, a moral component that determined the price. The price was to be established to promote social cooperation and mutual benefits rather than providing profit for only one side in the economic exchange.

Although we lack evidence that Warren was familiar with this sophisticated discussion, which was conducted mainly in Latin, his ideas place him within this philosophical tradition as he claimed that price should be based on other than only economic premises. Warren described the current state of economic exchange in which demand determined the price as "social cannibalism": a situation in which people would take advantage of their privileged position and act like cannibals, metaphorically eating those less privileged. To prove that price based on the supply-demand principle was unjust, Warren used the example of the water price for the thirsty travel[l]er in the desert. Warren claimed that water "costs nothing, or its cost is immaterial. If the travel[l]er was so thirsty that he would give a dollar for the water to him; and if the farmer were to charge this price, he would be acting upon the principle that '*The price of thing should be what it will bring*' which is motto and spirit of all the principle commerce of the word".[197] This was what Warren called "*disconnection*, a DISUNION between COST and *Value*".[198] To overcome this disconnection, he proposed to unify cost and value. Thus, for Warren, the value of commodities would become equal to the cost of production. That was how he coined his slogan "Cost the limit of price". The just reward for goods was the equivalent of its cost of production. Individuals in Warren's economic system voluntarily refused to accept any price higher than the cost of production to avoid "social cannibalism".

Making the cost of production the limit of price was essential but insufficient in achieving equality. He wanted to emphasise that work was the only title to

---

[194] Emil Kauder, *A History of Marginal Utility Theory* (Princeton, NJ: Princeton University Press, 1965) 5; Quoted by Murray N. Rothbard, *An Austrian Perspective on the History of Economic Thought: Volume 1* (Auburn, Alabama: Ludwig von Mises Institute, 2006) 142.

[195] J. Winthrop, John, J. K. Hosmer, *Winthrop's Journal, "History of New England" 1630-1649*, vol. 1 (New York: C. Scribner's Sons, 1908) 315.

[196] Winthrop, and Hosmer, *Winthrop's Journal* 318.

[197] Warren, *True Civilization* (1869) 41.

[198] Warren, *Equitable Commerce* (1846) 12.

profit. Warren strongly condemned any profit not related to work such as land speculation or the interest rate of loans, but also the rents of lands or buildings. Warren believed that eliminating money as the medium of exchange would help to make ties between work and the reward for work more visible.

In the entries from *Notebook D*, we can see some traces of constructing a more precise and fully elaborated structure of his system. However, his *Equitable Commerce* from 1846 fully exposed it most clearly. Warren asserted that different needs and demands were the source of all social problems. He boldly listed seven of the most important needs that must be satisfied to bring to life his ideal system:
"I. *THE PROPER, LEGITIMATE, AND JUST REWARD OF LABOR.*
II. *SECURITY OF PERSON AND PROPERTY.*
III. *THE GREATEST PRACTICABLE AMOUNT OF FREEDOM TO EACH INDIVIDUAL.*
IV. *ECONOMY IN THE PRODUCTION AND USES OF WEALTH.*
V. *TO OPEN THE WAY FOR EACH INDIVIDUAL TO THE POSSESSION OF LAND, AND ALL OTHER NATURAL WEALTH.*
VI. *TO MAKE THE INTERESTS OF ALL TO CO-OPERATE WITH AND ASSIST EACH OTHER, INSTEAD OF CLASHING WITH AND COUNTERACTING EACH OTHER.*
VII. *TO WITHDRAW THE ELEMENTS OF DISCORD, OF WAR, OF DISTRUST, AND REPULSION, AND TO ESTABLISH A PREVAILING SPIRIT OF PEACE, ORDER, AND SOCIAL SYMPATHY".*[199]

Moreover, he immediately proposed means of solution to these social problems. Securing individuality was the first and the most important instrument which determined all other means, including the sovereignty of every individual:
"I. INDIVIDUALITY.
S. SOVEREIGNTY OF EVERY INDIVIDUAL.
C. COST THE LIMIT OF PRICE,
M. CIRCULATING MEDIUM FOUNDED ON THE COST OF LABOR.
A. ADAPTATION OF THE SUPPLY TO THE DEMAND".[200]

Last, but not least, it is essential to keep in mind that under the system that provided the same reward for the same amount of labour for all people, women and children who participated in economic exchange received equal reward. He openly expressed that one hour of work of women and children has the same value as the work of men. He demanded equality for women more than a decade before Seneca Fall, and he consequently used the expression "he/she" in almost all of his writings more than a century before political correctness became common routine. Those facts, often neglected by his biographers, make him one of the most remarkable thinkers of the nineteenth century.

In his later writings, Warren elaborated his vision of an ideal social and economic system. The main problem, as he identified it, was the disconnect between

---

[199] Warren, *Equitable Commerce* (1846) 1.
[200] Warren, *Equitable Commerce* (1846) 1-2.

the cost and the value of things. The value of goods, according to Warren, should be equal to the cost of production. He envisioned making a profit by increasing prices as a reaction to increased demand as a form of "civilized cannibalism". An individual who participated in commerce should not concentrate on the growth of financial profits. The cost of production should be the only rational ground for a price.

Warren wrote that the *"SECURITY OF PERSON AND PROPERTY"* was one of the main social needs. He recognised the correlation between the security of a person and the security of his/her property. He maintained that it was not possible to provide security for a person without securing his/her right to acquire and hold private property.

Warren's thesis that cost was the only measure of the value of products may seem to question the existing economic order, especially the law of supply and demand. His ideas raised a vital question of whether there is any kind of order. An analysis of Warren's work suggests that there was a possibility of grounding society on purely conventional rules. However, it is also clearly visible that individuals taking part in the *Time Store* experiment were acting according to the *homo oeconomicus* rationality. The factor that provoked them to buy goods at the *Time Store* was their inclination to achieve greater profit. Consumers who were bound to work for Josiah Warren's *Time Store* received merchandise of a greater value than a possible financial gratification for this kind of work of an unskilled worker.

"The tendency of the issue of the labor-note by each individual, as a circulating medium, is to set up every one—man, woman, and child—upon a footing very nearly equal with regard to property; because, time being the principal element of the banking capital, and each one having the same amount of it, in every day and night, the difference between them will be chiefly in their different degrees of credit in the community, and their different natural capacities".[201]

Warren's convictions remained strong and unaffected. Just a few weeks before his death, he wrote to the editor of *Index* magazine to respond to the criticism. Explaining for the last time what the fair labor exchange would be and should be, he wrote: "For instance two men: one finds a brickbat, and the other picks up a diamond. You say that the cost principle requires that, the labor being the same, the one should exchange his diamond for the other's brickbat; entirely ignoring that the cost principle justifies him in demanding compensation, not only for the sacrifice of time and ease in picking up the jewel, but for the sacrifice made in parting with it. You do great injustice to the subject, too, when you imply that the cost principle requires any one to buy anything (like the brickbat) that is of no value to him: you seem to think that, because one accepts a principle, he is bound to accept any absurd application that any one chooses to make of it, however it may be distorted. But the natural sovereignty of each person will take care of this.

---

[201] Warren, and Andrews, *Practical Details* (1852) 83.

(…) I may buy a house that I have particularly desired, and be willing to pay more for it than its labor cost. If I do this cheerfully, all is well; but when the owner stretches his demands beyond what he knows to be compensation for his labor and sacrifices, he has entered into cannibalism [Here the manuscript abruptly ends; the tired hand, which at last found it impossible to execute the bidding of the tireless mind, rested from its toil forever.—Ed.]".[202] It was not that paying more than the cost of production was impossible. Rather, Warren put it in terms of morality. His *social cannibalism* had a strongly pejorative connotation. His principle was situated in the context of shaming and condemning those who took advantage of people's desire to obtain objects. Warren did not command anyone to behave in a certain manner. However, with his lofty opinion about human nature, he expected that we should behave not only properly but also honestly to keep up high standards.

---

[202] Josiah Warren, "Josiah Warren's Last Letter," *The Index* 30 Apr. 1874: 207.

CHAPTER 3

WARREN AND OTHERS

Josiah Warren is a remarkable American
J.S. Mill, The Collected Works of John Stuart Mill, vol. 1:
Autobiography and Literary Essays, *ed. J.M. Robson, J. Stillinger,*
(*University of Toronto Press, Toronto 1981*), 260.

As John Stuart Mill famously stated, Warren was a remarkable American. The aim of this chapter is to present Josiah Warren's intellectual framework in a broader perspective, comparing him with the following European philosophers: Robert Owen, John Stuart Mill and Pierre-Joseph Proudhon. In all three cases, the main purpose is to trace differences and similarities between Warren and others. Even though Warren openly admitted that he owed everything to Owen and perceived Owen as his intellectual father, some differences between them seem irreconcilable. In order to analyse them, it is essential to look closely at two debates: the one about the priority of individualistic or communal form of organising social life and – the second one contrasting private and common property systems of ownership.

Investigating relation between Mill and Warren, it seems to be the other way round as Mill gave credit to Warren for borrowing from him the notion of sovereignty. Therefore, it is crucial to look how those two thinkers perceived sovereignty, its possible limitations or limitations of its transfer as well as the role that pursuit of happiness played in their philosophical systems. In the last case, Warren and Proudhon were indifferent toward each other and it is even difficult to trace any signs of acknowledging the existence of one philosopher by the other. However, as they are both forerunners of anarchism, it is therefore indispensable to compare them. The most vital question in drawing such a comparison is how they attempted to ground the right to private property and what impact it might have had on their economic concepts.

3.1. Warren and Owen

3.1.1. Individuality versus communalism

The major difference between Warren and Owen was their vision of how to build a new society and on what grounds the social interaction should be constructed. The most vigorous debate with the most far reaching consequences was about the supremacy of individuals and their rights, needs and desires in shaping new social relations. More precisely, it was a debate about the supremacy of the community/society in deciding how new social relations would look like. This dispute between Warren and Owen could be understood as a conflict between individualism on the one hand and socialism or communism on the other.

Firstly, the problems with terms like *socialism* or *communism* which have been used in this debate are similar to the problems with the notion of individualism that were described in the first chapter. Applying all these notions to reality and those debates carried out in the early 1820s would be anachronistic. Also, Owen seemed to be as reluctant to use the term *socialism* as Warren was hostile towards the term *individualism*. Even though socialism had been associated with Owen and Owenism since the nineteenth century, it is essential to keep in mind that even Owen himself did not use the term *socialism*. During his activities in New Harmony (1825-1827) and earlier in England in the early 1820s, he preferred notions such as *co-operation, new vision of society* or *social system*.[203] However, Owen's vision of society was marked from the very first moment with a strong collectivist element. He placed great emphasis on this *social* factor, completely neglecting the role of the *individual*. Even if Owen did not support a social system based on private property, it must be observed that originally terms like *socialism* which were used by Owen and his contemporaries had been associated with social and collective aspects as opposed to the individualistic element; it is also worth to point out that at that time the notion of *socialism* did not refer to the mode of economic organisation where means of production, distribution, and exchange should be owned or regulated by the community as a whole.

Although Owen did not use the term *socialism* or *socialist*, the notion itself appeared for the first time in *The London Co-Operative Magazine*, the newspaper of the Owenite movement, in 1827, just after the collapse of the New Harmony community. An anonymous author wrote that "*The chief question (...) between the modern, (...) Political Economists, and the Communionists or Socialists, is whether it is more beneficial that this capital should be individual or in common)*".[204] Later, the notion of socialism appeared as a common name for different groups attempting to establish a social organisation based on common property. It was supposed to replace some particular names such *Fourierists* or *Owenists* with the more general term – *Socialism*.

In the American context, "'Socialism' was the antebellum catchword applied to any ideal community bent on replacing the greed syndrome with cooperation.

---

[203] Robert Owen, *A Discourse on a New System of Society: As Delivered in the Hall of Representatives of the United States, in Presence of the President of the United States, the President Elect, Heads of Departments, Members of Congress, &c. &c., on the 25th of February, 1825* (Washington: Gales & Seaton, 1825); see also John F.C. Harrison, *Quest for the New Moral World: Robert Owen and the Owenities in Britain and America* (New York: Scribner, 1969) 45.

[204] *Co-operation*, "The London Co-operative Magazine," 2.11 (Nov. 1827) 509.

In *The True Constitution of Government*, Andrews vaguely dovetails socialism with opposition to social injustice. When they get down to cases, such writers as Andrews and George Ripley do not think of socialism generically, as public control of productive property. To them it is a proprietary brand name for Fourierism, also known as Association, the secular form of communitarianism funded by joint-stock investment but operated collectively".[205] The 1840s were the first time when the notion of socialism became associated with the ideology of the former "Third State" represented by the middle class and the proletariat.[206] Also, during the 1820s and 1830s, the words *socialism* and *communism* were used interchangeably as denote doctrines stressing the need for radical social change and community of goods.

Despite this theoretical consideration – when and who created the term *socialism*, there is no doubt that the core of the Owenite system would be the communalistic form of organisation, which preceded mature socialism as we currently understand it. For Owen, the good of the individual corresponded with and, in many cases, would be even identical to the good of the community. Owen perceived the conflict between the individualistic vision and the communal vision of society as one of the most serious. The annihilation of the individual way of thinking and behaving became one of his major goals. In the address delivered upon his arrival at New Harmony Public Hall on April 27th, 1825, and published on the first page and in the first issue of the *New Harmony Gazette* in 1825, Owen made a significant statement, explaining the reasons for his arrival in America: "I come to this country, to introduce an entire new state of society; to change it from the ignorant, selfish system, to an enlightened, social system, which shall gradually unite all interests into one, and remove all cause for contest between individuals. The individual system has heretofore universally prevailed; and while it continues, the great mass of mankind must remain, as they comparatively are at present, ignorant, poor, oppressed, and, consequently, vicious, and miserable; and though it should last for numberless ages, virtue and happiness cannot be attained, nor can man, strictly speaking, become a rational being. Until the individual system shall be entirely abandoned, it will be useless to expect any substantial, permanent improvement in the condition of the human race; for this system ever has been, and must ever remain, directly opposed to universal charity, benevolence and kindness: and until the means were discovered, and can be brought into practice, by which universal charity, benevolence and kindness, can be made to pervade the heart and mind of every human being, a state of society in which 'peace on earth and good will to man' shall exist, must remain unknown and unenjoyed by mankind. These invaluable blessings can be obtained only under a social system; a system derived from an accurate knowledge of human nature, and of the circumstances by which it is, or may be governed".[207]

---

[205] Wunderlich, *Low Living* 125.

[206] Lorenz v. Stein, *Der Sozialismus und Kommunismus des heutigen Frankreichs* (Leipzig: O. Wigand, 1848), 67, 124, 137 and the following (the first edition is from the 1842).

[207] Robert Owen, "Address," *New Harmony Gazette*, 1 Oct. 1825: 1.

The guarantee of success, according to Owen, lay in the total annihilation of individual interests and desires. The main purpose of Owen's mission in American would be "(...) to change from the individual to the social system; from single families with separate interests, to communities of many families with one interest, cannot be accomplished at once; the change would be too great for the present habits of society; nor can it be effected in practice, except by those who have been long acquainted with each other, and whose habits, condition and sentiments, are similar; it becomes necessary, therefore, that some intermediate measures should be adopted, to enable all parties, with the least inconvenience, to change their individual, selfish habits, and to acquire the superior habits requisite to the social state; to proceed, if I may so express myself, to a halfway house on this new journey from poverty to wealth; from ignorance to intelligence; from anxiety to satisfaction of mind; from distrust of all, to confidence in every one; from bad habits and erroneous ideas, to good habits and a correct mode of thinking in all things; in short, from a combination of wretched, irrational circumstances, most unfavorable to every one, to new arrangements in unison with our nature, and most beneficial to all; and the only difficulty against which we should have to contend, will be while we shall have to remain in this halfway house, in which we shall have to give up the old habits acquired under the individual system, for the new habits requisite for the social and improved state of society for which we are now preparing".[208] Life was based on the rules that surpassingly allowed the unification of all interests, and by an unanimous action that removed all conflicts and discords.[209]

This approach was criticised by Warren, who in his first public article revealed a flaw in Owen's communal vision: "You perhaps already know, that Mr. Owen did not at the commencement, expect to assemble a sufficient number of persons for a society; in less than two years' time; but on the contrary, all the buildings were quite full in about two months from the beginning. This hasty and unexpected assemblage of persons from all parts of the earth; so widely different from each other, without any previous preparation for business, or for domestic accommodations, could not but produce confusion and counteraction at almost every step. Each one had his peculiar habits of thinking and acting, which had been produced by his *particular circumstances*, so that we were continually crossing each other at all points".[210]

Observing the failure of ordained unanimity and of removed individual preferences, Warren reached the conclusion that instead of eradicating them, they should be cherished and appraised. "It was perceived that as we were at all

---

[208] Owen, Adress 1.
[209] The Constitution of the Preliminary 2-3; Paul Brown, *Twelve Months in New-Harmony: Presenting a Faithful Account of the Principal Occurrences Which Have Taken Place There Within That Period; Interspersed with Remarks* (Cincinnati: W.H. Woodward, 1827) 23-28; Carmony, and Elliott, *New Harmony* 169-179.
[210] Warren, To the Friends of Social System (1 June 1827): 2.

times the creatures of surrounding circumstances, and as these combinations were always different, that every individual must be affected differently at different times, according to those circumstances; so that no one can with propriety dictate to another without his consent;— nor can any individual choose or dictate for himself beyond the present time, excepting in those things which are not liable to change. And it was seen that no individual can be secure or happy while he possesses power to control in any way his associates, or to interfere with them in their pursuit of happiness. But it was concluded that *society will lie prosperous and happy only in that proportion that each individual exercises that which his nature is continually demanding, the rigid of choosing or dictating at all times, and in all situations, the circumstances that have the power to affect him*".[211]

3.1.2. Private versus common property

One of the main goals established by the Owen community, except for the obvious provision of happiness,[212] was striving for a communal form of ownership. The first rules and regulations were stated in *A Constitution for a Preliminary Society*, probably drafted by Owen himself, which was adopted on May 1st, 1826. According to the rules, "Members were to furnish their own household and kitchen furniture as well as small tools such as axes and spades. Livestock owned by individuals would be taken over by the society, and the value of the animals would be placed to the credit of the previous owner if the society desired what was offered. Ownership of the town, buildings, and land remained with Robert Owen".[213] Owen was aware that the immediate implementation of the common property policy would be impossible, but even at this early stage there were many attempts for unification. "The living shall be upon equal terms for all, with the exceptions hereafter to be mentioned. In old age, in sickness, or when an accident occurs, care shall be taken of all parties, medical aid shall be afforded, and every attention shown to them that kindness can suggest. Each member shall, within a fixed amount in value, have the free choice of food and clothing".[214]

The very next year a new society was formed: *The New Harmony Community of Equality*, which succeeded the previous one. The constitution was adopted on February 5th, 1826 and provided more unification: "Equality of rights, uninfluenced by sex or condition, in all adults.

Equality of duties, modified by physical and mental conformation.

Cooperative union, in the business and amusements of life.

Community of property. (...)

---

[211] Warren, To the Friends of Social System (1 June 1827): 2.

[212] "The solo object of these Communities will be to procure for all their Members the greatest amount of happiness, to secure it to them, and to transmit it to their children to all latest posterity". The Constitution of the Preliminary 2.

[213] Carmony, and Elliott, *New Harmony* 168.

[214] The Constitution of the Preliminary 2.

The practice of economy, or of producing and using the best of everything in the most beneficial manner"[215]

However, "New Harmony under Owen's auspices never became a true communal society. Rather, it was a cooperative effort which had only the potential of becoming such a society"[216] Many attempts were taken to create it. The practical applications of such an undertaking were more complex and gloomy. In a letter by Thomas Pears to B. Bakewell written the following month, March 4th 1826, Pears complained that "The Constitution which was published, and which nearly all the members of the Preliminary Society signed, is now as nothing. The people here are divided into four classes: the Conscientious (...) another called the English Society; and within two days another which was originally composed of seven who made out a list which includes all the Literati (...) These resigned all membership, and many led by their example did the same. This has today been reconsidered [but many are still not], considered as Constitutionalists. (...) I would rather be a teaser (in the Glass House) than be here"[217]

The testimony of his wife, Sarah Pears, proved her distress and dissatisfaction: "In the first place, all our elder children, those whom we expected to be comfort and consolation and support in our old age, are to be taken away from us, at an age, too, when they so peculiarly require the guardian care of their parents; and are to be placed in large boarding houses. The single males and females above the age of fourteen are to live together in one house, over which there is to be one married woman to superintend. (...) Instead of our own dear children each housekeeper is to receive two more families, one of which will have a child under two years old. The rest will be at the boarding school. These three families are each to live in community, and take the cooking by turns. We have already got one family with us, but as the people are leaving the Society very fast, I hope it will not be necessary to take a third. If it is, however, I shall prefer going into one of their miserable log cabins to being crowded so thick. I have hitherto been able to do very little besides sew and take care of my baby; and my health is now, as well as my poor baby's, extremely delicate. How I am to go through cooking, washing and scrubbing I really do not know. But I know were I to consider this world only, I would rather, far rather, that Mr. Owen would shoot me through the head. My mind is absolutely in such a state that I am almost incapable of doing anything, and next week expect my daughters will be taken away from me. If I am sick I cannot have my own daughters to nurse me, but must be taken to the hospital to be taken care of by strangers. I know not really how I can write such things and keep my senses"[218]

---

[215] "Constitution of the New Harmony Community of Equality," *New Harmony Gazette* 15 Feb. 1826: 161.

[216] Carmony, and Elliott, *New Harmony* 169.

[217] Thomas Pears and Sarah Pears and Thomas C. Pears, *New Harmony, an Adventure in Happiness: Papers of Thomas and Sarah Pears* (Indianapolis: Indiana historical Society, 1933) 67.

[218] T. Pears, S. Pears, T. C. Pears, *New Harmony* 72-73.

This passage provides a clear proof that the communion of needs and goals, similarly to communal property, was not achieved. Therefore, we might better comprehend Warren's reservation toward such implemented communalism. Warren's economic system was based on *"security of persons and property"*. His opinion on private property was shaped during his Owenite period, parallel with his convictions of the importance of individualism. Warren, like others in New Harmony, blamed the malfunction of the colony on property relations among the colonists. He wrote: "Let us bear in mind that during the great experiments in New Harmony in 1825 and 1826, every thing went delightfully on, except pecuniary affairs! We should, no doubt, have succeeded but for property considerations. But then the experiments never would have been commenced but for property considerations. It was to annihilate social antagonism by a system of *common property*, that we undertook the experiments at all".[219]

Warren became convinced that the implementation of a common property system would not correct the unjust distribution of private property. However, at the same time, he did not want to abandon the Owenite egalitarian idea. As a result, a barter exchange of goods and services based on the labour for labour principle was supposed to ensure the more equal distribution of commodities. Observing the malfunctions evident in the Owenite New Harmony, he believed that collectivism and common property were the main reasons behind the community's failure. As he concluded in his Notebook: "In the experiments of communities of common property attempted in New Harmony the word assumed a very important position. It was one of the cornerstones of the whole superstructure, but it was a different thing with almost every different person. One applied so as to prescribe the same amount of value to each member for clothing and food leaving him free to choose the kind according to taste etc. while another insisted that the word fairly prescribed the same kind, color and make of clothing and insisted on uniformity of dress as one of the most necessary external signs of that equality of condition desirable among men".[220] This lack of unanimity among members of New Harmony, and the strong disappointment in the communal form of ownership led Warren to advocate for a system of private property based on individual rights and sovereignty for all individuals. Warren believed that "[t]he Sovereignty of every one over his own person and property and other interests, demands that we should determine what are the rightful claims of every one to property".[221] Elaborating further on the notion of the rightful claim, he believed that people were entitled to "the whole produce or results of his/her own labor".[222]

---

[219] Warren, and Andrews, *Practical Details* (1852) 71.
[220] Warren, *Notebook D* 65.
[221] Josiah Warren, *Periodical Letter*, 1.2 (Aug. 1854): 23.
[222] Warren, and Andrews, *Practical Details* (1852) 13-14.

3.1.3. Labour notes and co-operatives

Gregory Claeys pointed out an existing debate about who was the first inventor of labour notes and barter exchange of goods as a just reward for labour. Claeys referred to a piece published by Robert Owen in the *New Harmony Gazette* on December 12th, 1827, announcing the labour for labour exchange.[223] Frank Podmore attributed the invention to Warren and pointed out the impact he had made on Owen to fully developed this concept: "From the fourth quarterly report of the British Association for promoting Co-operative Knowledge, published early in 1830, we learn that Owen, no doubt with Warren's experiment in his mind, had advocated the use of labour notes at the Greville Street Bazaar".[224] Claeys disagreed with Podmore's diagnosis and argued that "Owen clearly conceived it several years earlier".[225] Claeys admitted that "Warren did communicate directly with British co-operators, e.g. *British Co-operator*, no. 3 (June 1830), 62".[226] Even if Claeys was correct and Owen had conceived the idea prior to Warren, the latter offered its earlier practical exposition: because his *Time Store* had been open from May 1827, it had even preceded Owen's communication in the *New Harmony Gazette* in December 1827. Only Lockwood attributed some early and vague ideas of the labour note to Owen who "proposed the establishment of 'banks of real wealth,' with a rather indefinite method of transacting business. The new medium of exchange must have the power of expansion and contraction, as the value of material expanded or contracted".[227] However, Lockwood did not attribute this to the first or second visit of Robert Owen in New Harmony. Later on, even Lockwood, as the first researcher ever, stated that "from Josiah Warren, who founded the New Harmony 'Time store,' and originated a system of 'labor notes,' Robert Owen derived the central idea of the great labor cooperative societies of Great Britain, which constitute the most successful labor movement of the last century".[228] Also Schuster repeated this claim "that Owen derived from Warren the central idea of the great labor cooperative societies of Great Britain, which constitute one of the most successful movements of the last century in that country".[229]

Perhaps the most accurate interpretation of the events was offered by Bailie, who observed that "While it was Robert Owen who, in a plan devised in 1820 to relieve the industrial woes of Ireland, first proposed the use of labor notes, yet the idea had not been put in practice until Warren, in his original way, successfully

---

[223] Geroge Claeys, *Machinery, Money, and the Millennium: From Moral Economy to Socialism, 1815-1860*. Princeton, N.J: Princeton Univ. Press, 1987) 206.

[224] Frank Podmore, *Robert Owen: a biography*, vol. 2 (London: Hutchinson, 1906) 404.

[225] Claeys, *Machinery* 206.

[226] Claeys, *Machinery* 206.

[227] George B. Lockwood, *The New Harmony Communities* (Marion: Chronicle, 1902) 81 (p. 64 in the edition from 1905).

[228] Lockwood, *The New Harmony Communities* 14.

[229] Schuster, *Native American* 95.

carried it out".[230] The same opinion was shared by Agnes Inglis, who wrote that while "Robert Owen is given the credit of conceiving of the plan of Equal Exchange and Time Notes, Josiah Warren is given the credit of demonstrating this idea in his TIME STORE of Cincinnati, Ohio, in 1827-1830, after returning from New Harmony, where he associated with Robert Owen, and got many ideas".[231] It is not possible to determine whether Warren or Owen invented the labour for labour exchange idea, but it is definitely possible to establish that Warren must have been its first practitioner.

Moreover, there is one more piece of evidence for Warren's transatlantic connections during the early 1830s, except of that mentioned by Claeys. W. Bryan in his communication to the *British Co-operator* from July 26th 1830 from New York City reported: "I had made arrangements with Josiah Warren of Cincinnati, who was here a few weeks, to open my store as the depot for a Labour for Labour Association; but on re-considering the subject, we concluded society was not yet sufficiently interested in the subject to enable us to succeed without a very considerable loss of time, more than our circumstances could bear. So we have relinquished the idea until a more favourable opportunity; and he has joined a small party in Stark county, Ohio, to carry the principles of labour for labour into practice".[232]

Agnes Inglis believed that Warren had made a personal impact on Owen to put the labour for labour idea into practice. "Running his TIME STORE there in Cincinnati, Josiah Warren interested many people in It. Robert Owen was in Cincinnati, in 1829 and without doubt saw Josiah Warren and his Time Store. We can say 'without doubt' because it would seem most unlikely that these two warm friends did not meet at that time, and it would seem most unlikely that Owen was not desirous of seeing his own idea in working form. In Cincinnati, for a debate, [in] the spring of 1829, Robert Owen returned to England the latter part of that year of 1829 leaving America for many years. In England, he started his activities and among them his 'EQUAL EXCHANGE BAZAAR or MAGAZINE'".[233]

Furthermore, some indirect evidence of the interests of Owen and the advocates of the Owenite movement might be found in the article published in the *Free Enquirer* by Robert. L. Jennings, who was at that time editor of the *Free Enquirer*[234] entitled "On Social Equality" from May 27th 1829. Jennings campaigned for the formation of cooperative associations "based upon the rational foundation of free and universal enquiry, and on the principle that the action of individuals,

---

[230] Bailie, *Josiah Warren* 11.

[231] University of Michigan, Labadie Collection, Agnes Inglis Papers, Box 32, Research and notes.

[232] Bryan, Untitled letter 160.

[233] University of Michigan, Labadie Collection, Agnes Inglis Papers, Box 32, Research and notes.

[234] R.L. Jennings remained an editor till May 1830.

whether their own happiness or misery is concerned, if not productive of misery to others, is the business of none but themselves".[235]

Warren himself clearly denied inventing labour notes stating in 1848 in his periodical *The Peaceful Revolutionist* that "[t]he idea of labour notes was suggested by Robert Owen in 1826 as a medium of exchange between Communities at New Harmony".[236] Some of the labour notes printed and signed by Warren himself are still in the Historic New Harmony Archive.[237] The system of *labour notes* played an important part in the process of enhancing the level of equality. Time was the only measurement of equality, where one hour of work was exchanged for another participant's hour of work. The time dedicated to producing a commodity became more visible and was clearly put on the *labour notes*. When the time became commonly accepted measurement, the equal exchange of time prevented any form of speculation and injustice.

At the same time, Warren combined his vision of individual private property with the statement that "all natural wealth should be common".[238] In the state of nature, the earth and all natural wealth belongs to everyone, are *res communis*. All natural resources "or the gifts of nature become accessible to all, for they are not subject to price; only what an individual adds to these gifts is an appropriate basis for price (...) natural resources become available to all for the cost of the labour necessary to dig them out of the ground, prepare them for use, and deliver them to the buyer".[239]

According to Warren, extra profit exceeding labour was inappropriate and unjust. However, the idea of natural resources owned by everyone did not exclude the possibility of an original appropriation, similar to the Lockean appropriation expressed in his famous *Second Treaty on Government*.[240] On the contrary, Warren was even reluctant to formulate any proviso similar to the Lockean proviso because from his perspective of the early nineteenth century Midwesterner natural resources seemed to be endless. Therefore, there was no point in establishing any limitation over appropriation.

The opposition to Owen's collectivist ideas and the consequences of the New Harmony episode convinced Warren that individualism was essential. Warren's philosophy not only emphasised the importance of the individual, but it also hold that only individual human beings are a subject worthy of study. After New Harmony and other socio-economical experiments, in 1846 Warren published his first accomplished masterpiece: *Equitable Commerce, A New Development of Principles As Substitutes For Laws And Governments, For The Harmonious*

---

[235] R.L.J. "On Social Equality" *Free Enquirer* 27 May 1829: 245-247.

[236] *Peaceful Revolutionist*, II (May, 1848): 6, 14.

[237] I would like to thank Amanda Bryden for pointing out the accurate location. Initially I misplaced Warren's labour notes in the Working Men's Institute Library.

[238] Warren, *Notebook D* 122. My emphasis.

[239] Warren, *True Civilization* (1869) 74-75.

[240] John Locke, *Two Treaties about Government*, § 27-29, any edition.

Adjustment And Regulation of the Pecuniary, Intellectual, And Moral Intercourse of Mankind Proposed as Elements of New Society. The first sentence reveals that the aim of his work and "the foundation of whole subject, is – the Study of Individuality, or the practice of mentally discriminating, dividing, separating, or disconnecting persons, things, and events, according to their individual peculiarities".[241] From that point, Warren's philosophical system was focused on identification and analysis of particularities, not elements that are common to all people.

Warren's vision of private property led him to a rejection of society, but also to a rejection of any government that might limit individual rights. Warren claimed that "[i]t leaves everyone in undisturbed possession of his or her natural and proper sovereignty over its own person, time, property and responsibilities; & no one is acquired or expected to surrender any 'portion' of his natural liberty by joining any society whatever; nor to become in any way responsible for the acts or sentiments of anyone but himself; nor is there any arrangement by which even the whole body can exercise any government over the person, time property or responsibility of a single individual".[242] This places Warren's ideas close to those of individualist anarchists.

3.2. Warren and Mill

3.2.1. Sovereignty

While Mill openly admitted that he had borrowed the notion of sovereignty from Warren, it is worth investigating the ways in which these two thinkers constructed the concept of sovereignty of the individual, on what ground it was built and what might be its possible limitations. Warren used the term "sovereignty of individual" for the first time in the *Peaceful Revolutionist* in February 1833. Although he did not provide any precise definition, the term was clearly used in the context of liberty and inalienable rights. "LIBERTY is safe, and the only safe principle to which we can pledge ourselves. If it be objected that this Liberty is unattainable, and that great national objects could not be attained where such latitude was encouraged, I reply that there can be no national object greater that the national happiness – that this, as I understand it, consist of the happiness of the *individuals* who composed the nation, and that individual happiness consists in nothing so much as in the LIBERTY of person and property. If this is unattainable in large masses, it shows us one *circumstance* with which we have contend, and prove that *society will have to dissolve its imaginary masses and combinations and RESOLVE ITSELF INTO INDIVIDUALIS, before liberty can be anything but a word*".[243]

---

[241] Warren, *Equitable Commerce* (1846) 3.
[242] Josiah Warren, *Manifesto* (New Harmony: 1841).
[243] Josiah Warren, "Of our state difficulties," *Peaceful Revolutionist* 1.2 (Feb. 1833): 6.

Understood in this way, liberty can only be defined, acquired and sustained on an individual level. Therefore, Warren compels us to dissolve society, or – as he called it – the "imaginary masses". Particular differences that are manifested into particularities of individual character must be secured by the right of an individual to make any decision regarding his or her life. Warren blamed the collectivist vision of the "imaginary masses": "I say its *imaginary* masses, for, notwithstanding that the ingenuity of man has been exerted to the utmost, and that interest, fears, hopes, persuasion fraud and force have been brought to bear upon human motives to make men think, feel, decide and act alike; and ages have passed away in witnessing and suffering the calamitous consequences, yet, at this late day, it remains for us to attract attention to the *INDIVIDULIATY OF CHARACTER* observable throughout the human race – *to the various effects which the same circumstances have been different, and to the different effects produced by the same circumstance upon the same person at different times*".[244] The individualist approach led Warren to recognise the good only in the self-interests of the individual. In the process of searching for happiness, the good comes from each person's individual ability to govern himself or herself. Therefore, for Warren the source of evil would be the vision of general good, public good, or social good imposed on individual modes of life.[245]

According to Warren, sovereignty is not only grounded in individual, pre-political rights that existed prior to the foundation of any social or state organisation and structure. This notion of sovereignty is rooted in the ontological concept of the human being and their epistemological abilities; it is embedded in our senses, and any external imposition upon the individual would be impossible. This led Warren to the conclusion that "[t]his *individuality of persons and cases*, no power within our knowledge can destroy or control; and the facts that 'no one has any power to like which is disagreeable' and that every one is compelled like that which is agreeable', teach us, as we love our own happiness, to respect every one's individual feelings and Liberty, and not to make any social arrangement which compel us to violate them. These views have so far resulted in the conclusion that the happiness of society would best be promoted by awarding to each and every individual. SOVEREIGNITY OF HIS OR HER PERSON AND PROPERTY, AN EQUIVALENT WHEN THAT PROPERTY IS EXCHANGED".[246]

Almost a decade later, Warren returned to this concept in a brief work published as the *Gazette of Equitable Commerce* in 1842 in New Harmony. "To this many replies might be made but we shall not judge before trial-Justice has always been presented to us in such an offensive attitude that we have been driven to resist rather than obey her haughty and imperious commands. When it shall be

---

[244] Warren, Of our state 6.

[245] A, Butler, *Josiah Warren, Peaceful Revolutionist*, Ball State University 1978, UMI 7919881, p. 4-5.

[246] Warren, Of our state 6.

admitted that it is one part of justice to acknowledge that the SOVEREIGNTY OF EACH INDIVIDUAL is our first, greatest and most *'inalienable'* right, (derived from the unconquerable laws *of* our Nature) then, we shall have *no commands* to resist, and her wise & saving councils may obtain a hearing".[247] Here Warren emphasised even more precisely the correlation between liberty and sovereignty, with sovereignty being a necessary element guaranteeing the liberty of individuals. Sovereignty is put in third place in the plan demanding "III. To RESTORE THE NATURAL LIBERTY OF THE CITIZEN. **OR,** TO ESTABLISH THE **Sovereignty of every individual** OVER HER OR HIS PERSON, TIME, PROPERTY AND RESPONSIBILITIES".[248]

In *Equitable Commerce*, Warren explained the concept of sovereignty in a more detailed manner and showed its consequences while he formulated and defined sovereignty as the supreme law unto himself. "From the study of this Individuality, together with our natural instinct for self-preservation, I draw the conclusion, that each individual should be at all times free to differ from every other in thought, feeling, word, and deed; and free to differ from himself, or to change from time to time; in other words, that every one is constituted by nature to be at all times, SOVEREIGN OF HIMSELF OR HERSELF, and of every thing that constitutes a part of his or her Individuality. That society to be harmonious and successful, must be so constituted that there shall be no demand for an outward show of conformity or uniformity—that no person must have any power over the: persons or interests of others; but that every one shall be at all times, the SUPREME 'LAW UNTO HIMSELF'".[249]

"I will not now delay to detail the reasonings which led to the conclusion that SOCIETY MUST BE so CONSTRUCTED AS TO PRESERVE THE **SOVEREIGNTY OF EVERY INDIVIDUAL** INVIOLATE. *That it must avoid all combinations and connections of persons and interests, and all other arrangements, which will not leave every individual at all times at* LIBERTY *to dispose of his or her person, and time, and property, in any manner in which his or her feelings or judgment may dictate,* WITHOUT INVOLVING THE PERSONS OR INTERESTS OF OTHERS.

That there must be

Individuality of Interests,

Individuality of Responsibilities,

Individuality in the deciding power; and, in one sense,

Individuality of action".[250]

In the early 1870s, Warren put forward more precisely that this right of individual sovereignty was designed only for the agents – rational individuals that

---

[247] Josiah Warren, *Gazette of Equitable Commerce* (1842): 3.

[248] Warren, Gazette of equitable 6.

[249] Warren, *Equitable Commerce* (1846) 10-11.

[250] Warren, and Andrews, *Practical Details* (1852) 13. 3.

were able to take decisions regarding their life. "That, every person of sane mind and capable of self-support is rightful SOVEREIGN of his or her own *person, property* and *responsibilities*, and has a right to repel, and to combine with others to repel, all aggressors upon these SOVEREIGN RIGHTS—be they individuals, or organizations called governments; but to go beyond this, is to become, in turn, aggressive and criminal".[251] However, in Warren's philosophy children were also perceived as agents. Warren believed that a child could make a decision and bear consequences in the same way as an adult would. For Mill, however, the definition of an agent is much narrower. Mill insisted that "[i]t is, perhaps, hardly necessary to say that this doctrine is meant to apply only to human beings in the maturity of their faculties. We are not speaking of children, or of young persons below the age which the law may fix as that of manhood or womanhood".[252] This was one of the essential difference between Mill's and Warren's perception of sovereignty.

3.2.2. Possible limitations of sovereignty

John Stuart Mill opened his famous chapter IV *Of the limits to the authority of society over the individual* by asking "WHAT, then, is the rightful limit to the sovereignty of the individual over himself? Where does the authority of society begin? How much of human life should be assigned to individuality, and how much to society"?[253] Even though Warren did not pose this question explicitly, he had thought about it. Both thinkers offered quite different answers, even though they had common starting point: the defence of individual rights.

Mill declared in the chapter IV of his iconic piece *On Liberty* that sovereignty is absolute and unlimited, but only in this narrow sphere where it regards one's rights over himself or herself: "In the part which merely concerns himself, his independence is, of right, absolute. Over himself, over his own body and mind, the individual is sovereign".[254] Thus, it might appear that sovereignty of the individual would be Mill's highest goal and such sovereignty would remain unrestrained and unlimited.

However, this diagnosis is relevant only when we think about the sovereignty placed in the context of an individual decision relevant to the decision maker. When we examine carefully the entire passage, one will notice that for Mill sovereignty is set in the social context, when our decisions might influence lives of others. "The object of this Essay is to assert one very simple principle as entitled to govern absolutely the dealings of society with the individual in the way of compulsion and control, whether the means used be physical force in the

---

[251] Josiah Warren, *Political Platform for the Coming Party* (Boston: publisher not identified. Possibly Warren himself, 1871) 1.

[252] John Stuart Mill, *On Liberty: The Subjection of Women* (New York: Holt, 1879) 23-24, Collected works, vol. XVIII, 224. (page reference will be given to both: Holt edition, and collected works of J.S. Mill).

[253] Mill, *On Liberty* (1879) 133; Collected works, vol. XVIII, 276.

[254] Mill, *On Liberty* (1879) 23-24, Collected works, vol. XVIII, 224.

form of legal penalties, or the moral coercion of public opinion. That principle is, that the sole end for which mankind are warranted, individually or collectively, in interfering with the liberty of action of any of their number, is self-protection. That the only purpose for which power can be rightfully exercised over any member of a civilized community, against his will is to prevent harm to others. (…) To justify that, the conduct from which it is desired to deter him must be calculated to produce evil to some one else. The only part of the conduct of any one, for which he is amenable to society, is that which concerns others. In the part which merely concerns himself, his independence is, of right, absolute. Over himself, over his own body and mind, the individual is sovereign".[255]

This brought up the questions about Mill's paternalism. There is no doubt that Mill was in favour of the active participation of the state in the life of the citizens to the extent that "Not only does the State undertake to decide disputes, it takes precautions beforehand that disputes may not arise".[256] The following famous example might be used as evidence of Mill's paternalism: "If either a public officer or anyone else saw a person attempting to cross a bridge which had been ascertained to be unsafe, and there was no time to warn him of his danger, they might seize him and turn him back, without any real infringement of his liberty, for liberty consists in doing what one desires, and he does not desire to fall into the river".[257]

This is why many researchers acknowledged the fact that Mill permitted relatively broad interference into the sphere of personal liberty. However, as John Gray observed, this might be deceiving: "Mill conceives of his principle as allowing the state and society to limit a man's liberty so as to protect him from the damaging consequences of his own ignorance or delusion, wherever the circumstances of the case give good reason for supposing that his uninformed or misinformed choice did not correspond to the choice he would have made had he understood clearly the situation in which he found himself".[258] Amy Gutman and Dennis Thompson pointed out that there were some critics who "have objected that the distinction between self-regarding and other-regarding actions is pointless: almost any citizen's actions affect other citizens and often society as a whole. If you harm yourself, you harm others who depend on you; if you act immorally, you may tempt others to act immorally".[259] Therefore, the classification into a justified governmental intervention (when a citizen's action harms other people) and un unjustified governmental intervention (when a person harms only himself or herself) is artificial.

---

[255] Mill, *On liberty* (1879) 23-24, Collected works, vol. XVIII, 224.

[256] John Stuart Mill, *Principles of Political Economy with some of their Applications to Social Philosophy*, (London: Longmans, Green and Co., 1909) 799.

[257] Mill, *On liberty* (1879) 171, Collected works, vol. XVIII, 294.

[258] John Gray, *Mill on Liberty: A Defence* (London: Routledge, 1996) 91.

[259] Amy Gutman, Dennis Thomson, *Democracy and Disagreement* (Cambridge: Harvard University Press, 1996) 231.

Mill was aware of the paradox and openly admitted: "How (it may be asked) can any part of the conduct of a member of society be a matter of indifference to other members? No person is an entirely isolated being".[260] Nevertheless, he was not able to provide a solution to this problem while Warren achieved this goal by demanding disassociation and separation of all interests based on his hyper- -individualistic system. Moreover, for Mill, it was possible to delegate individual sovereignty; and with the acceptance of such a delegation, a people's representatives would constitute a parliament that was perceived by Mill as the "the nation's Committee of Grievances, and its Congress of Opinions".[261] The government should not only provide protection, but indtroduce taxation in order to be able to perform its duties. Although Mill concluded that while interfering with individual liberty the government should always be self-restrained, his acceptance of such interference was quite extensive. When an individual "neither violates any specific duty to the public, nor occasions perceptible hurt to any assignable individual except himself; the inconvenience is one which society can afford to bear, for the sake of the greater good of human freedom. If grown persons are to be punished for not taking proper care of themselves, I would rather it were for their own sake, than under pretence of preventing them from impairing their capacity of rendering to society benefits which society does not pretend it has a right to exact. But I cannot consent to argue the point as if society had no means of bringing its weaker members up to its ordinary standard of rational conduct, except waiting till they do something irrational, and then punishing them, legally or morally, for it. Society has had absolute power over them during all the early portion of their existence: it has had the whole period of childhood and non-age in which to try whether it could make them capable of rational conduct in life".[262]

Considering the question of a government's interference into individual liberty, Mill asserts that it should always restrict itself to doing only what is necessary. Firstly, a government should prohibit and punish individual behaviour that harms other people, such as coercion, fraud or negligence. Secondly, should work toward limiting or even eliminating the great amount of energy being spent on harming one nation by another. Thirdly, a government should turn such destructive behaviour into improving human faculties, namely, transforming the powers of nature so that they serve the greatest physical and moral good. Finally, Mill proposes that governments should adopt a laissez-faire policy so that they might abstain from interfering with individual choice and grant unconstrained freedom to people, who should be able to pursue their happiness without restrictions.

Another possibility in limiting governmental authority would be "the greatest dissemination of power consistent with efficiency, but the greatest possible centralization of information and diffusion of it from the center",[263] and Mill

---

[260] Mill, *On liberty* (1879) 142, Collected works, vol. XVIII, 280.
[261] Mill, "Consideration of representative government" Collected Works, vol. XIX, 432.
[262] Mill, *On liberty* (1879) 146, Collected works, vol. XVIII, 282.
[263] Mill, *On liberty* 201, Collected works, vol. XVIII, 309.

expected that in contrast to its limited "actual power", the central governmental organ of this function would issue "advice" which "would naturally carry much authority".[264] As it might be observed, there are some limitations to Mill's concept of sovereignty. "The problem is to make the fitting adjustment between the independence of the individual and social control. How shall we justify compulsion and control, that is, physical force, in the form of legal penalties, and the moral coercion of public opinion? The answer is simple and clear. Society has no right to interfere with that part of a person's conduct that concerns only himself, and in which society, as distinguished from the individual, has, if any, only an indirect interest; in that his independence is of right absolute: he is sovereign over his own body and mind. Society has jurisdiction only over that part of human life that chiefly interests society".[265]

Mill provided so many exceptions that permitted encroachment of individual rights defined in terms of absolute sovereignty that it might have been impossible for Warren to recognise his own influence on Mill's vision. Warren did not put forward any scenario in which individual sovereignty might be limited. There is no possibility of clashes of rights among individuals. Warren believed in the power of modesty and self-restraint. Numerous individuals would not act to violate the rights of others due to selfish motivations – people need the assistance of others to pursue their goals and achieve happiness, therefore they would not encroach on the rights of others. In such a perception of human nature, there is no space for any reasonable motivation for limiting the sovereignty of the individual. Such a construction is a visible pillar of Warren's anarchism. Individuals do not need to limit or transfer their power. What is more, they will not be subdued – even to statutory law.

The government has been established to provide security for persons and property but fails to achieve those goals. Therefore, individuals do not have a duty to obey the laws established by the government, especially as those laws do not recognise individual particularities and are based on generalisations. Warren argued that "Laws and governments are professedly instituted for the security of person and property but, they have never accomplished that object. Even to this day every newspaper shows that they commit more crimes upon persons and property and contribute more to their insecurity than all criminals put together. The greatest crime which can be committed against society and which causes poverty and lays the foundation of almost all other crimes, is the monopoly of the soil; this has not only been permitted but protected or perpetuated by every government of modern times up to the last accounts from the congress of the United States. For this enormous crime, according to the spirit of all law, these legislators ought to be severely punished; but the principles of law are false, every act of every legislator

---

[264] Mill, *On liberty* 202, Collected works, vol. XVIII, 309.
[265] Frank Thilly, "The Individualism of John Stuart Mill," *The Philosophical Review* 32 (Jan. 1923): 1-13.

has been an *effect* over which he could have no control while the *causes* existed; this is the only ground upon which they can rationally be acquitted, and the same would protect all other criminals from being lawfully murdered and should teach legislators to *remove causes* rather than spend the peoples' money in *punishing effects.* (...).Laws cannot be adapted to the individuality of cases, and if they could, laws are language which is subject to different interpretations according to the individuals who are appointed to administer them, therefore, it is individuals rather than laws that govern. Every election illustrates this: we are told that our destinies depend on the election of this or that man to office! why? this shows that it is m e n not laws or principles that govern society. There is an individuality among judges and jurors as among all other persons; so that he whom one judge or jury would acquit, another would condemn: (...) Citizens cannot know today what will be lawful tomorrow; laws made this year are unmade the next and their repeal is often our only intimation that they existed. All these uncertainties must exist even when laws are framed with the greatest wisdom and administered with the purest devotedness to the public good without the least tinge of personal feeling or private interest, provided such phenomena are to be found, but every newspaper that comes to hand convinces me that such are not found even in the proportion of ten to the population of Sodorn; but that, notwithstanding all that revolutions have cost the world, laws and governments still are what they always have been viz. p u b l i c   m e a n s   u s e d   f o r   p r i v a t e   e n d s".[266]

In his *Practical Details* Warren stated once again that "If this be true, then all systems of government, and all laws, and all powers which assume control over or claim a right to govern any one against his or her will or inclination, ARE FALSE! The foundation of this error is generally laid in the very first step toward the organization of society, in admitting as a dogma, that *'when we enter into society we surrender a portion of our natural liberty.'* This has been admitted without sufficient scrutiny, and has been built upon in every possible mode; but the building has no sooner fallen and crushed its thousands, than another is erected in its place to work similar ruin; while the subtle rottenness of the foundation remains hidden, unseen, unexamined, *unmoved".*[267] Thus, even if Warren, due to myriad reasons, did not want to procure a self-declaration of being an anarchist, his inability to compromise in terms of individual sovereignty definitely made him one of the "black flag comrades".

3.2.3. Happiness

The essential common element in Mill's and Warren's philosophies, except for the notion of individual sovereignty used by both thinkers, is the notion of happiness. "Actions are right in proportion as they tend to promote happiness,

---

[266] Warren, A Brush 14.
[267] Warren, and Andrews, *Practical Details* (1852) 77.

wrong as they tend to produce the reverse of happiness. By happiness is intended pleasure, and the absence of pain; by unhappiness, pain, and the privation of pleasure".[268] "By "pleasure" and "pain", Mill does not mean only "bodily" sensations. His definition also includes "higher" pleasures such as those "of the intellect, the feelings and imagination, and of the moral sentiments".[269] As Henry R. West noticed, "Utilitarianism is thus a *hedonistic* theory (from the Greek word for "pleasure"), but its hedonism is to be understood in this broad sense to include all mental or psychological pleasures and pains, not just those of the bodily senses".[270]

In his definition of utilitarianism, Mill concludes that "[b]y happiness is intended pleasure, and the absence of pain; by unhappiness, pain, and the privation of pleasure. To give a clear view of the moral standard set up by the theory, much more requires to be said (...)But these supplementary explanations do not affect the theory of life on which this theory of morality is grounded—namely, that pleasure, and freedom from pain, are the only things desirable as ends; and that all desirable things (which are as numerous in the utilitarian as in any other scheme) are desirable either for the pleasure inherent in themselves, or as means to the promotion of pleasure and the prevention of pain".[271]

There is no evidence to what extent Mill was familiar with Warren's philosophy and writings. It is rather unlikely that Warren's works, associating pain with undesirable actions and pleasure with desirable ones, that had been published in local Midwestern American newspapers in the late 1820s, circulated in London. However, there is no doubt that such connection existed between Mill and Jeremy Bentham. Bentham's philosophy therefore might have been the link between Mill and Warren, and it is highly probable that Warren knew Bentham's theory. What Bentham laid out in the opening of his classical *An Introduction to the Principles of Morals and Legislation* was that "[n]ature has placed mankind under the governance of two sovereign masters, *pain* and *pleasure*. It is for them alone to point out what we ought to do, as well as to determine what we shall do. On the one hand the standard of right and wrong, on the other the chain of causes and effects, are fastened to their throne. They govern us in all we do, in all we say, in all we think: every effort we can make to throw off our subjection, will serve but to demonstrate and confirm it. In words a man may pretend to abjure their empire: but in reality he will remain subject to it all the while. The *principle of utility*[272]

---

[268] John Stuart Mill, *Utilitarianism, Collected Works of John Stuart Mill: 10*. John M. Robson (Ed.) Indianapolis, Ind: Liberty Fund, 2006 229.

[269] Mill, *Utilitarianism*, 210. Cf. Necip Fikri Alican *Mill's Principle of Utility: A Defense of John Stuart Mill's Notorious Proof* (Amsterdam: Rodopi, 1994).

[270] Henry West ed., *Blackwell Guide to Mill's Utilitarianism* (Malden, MA: Blackwell Pub, 2006) 1-2.

[271] Mill, *Utilitarianism* 210.

[272] "To this denomination has of late been added, or substituted, the greatest happiness or greatest felicity principle: this for shortness, instead of saying at length that principle which states the greatest happiness of all those whose interest is in question, as being the right and proper, and only right and proper and universally desirable, end of human action: of human action in every

recognizes this subjection, and assumes it for the foundation of that system, the object of which is to rear the fabric of felicity by the hands of reason and of law. Systems which attempt to question it, deal in sounds instead of sense, in caprice instead of reason, in darkness instead of light".[273] The only version of the utility principle that fulfills this requirement is the Greatest Happiness Principle: "In the eyes of every impartial arbiter, writing in the character of legislator, and having exactly the same regard for the happiness of every member of the community in question as for that of every other, the greatest happiness of the greatest number of the members of that same community can not but be recognized in the character of the right and proper, and sole right and proper, end of government".[274]

When we compare the roles that *happiness* played for such utilitarian philosophers as Bentham or Mill, it is clear that happiness would be a measurement of the axiological value of moral theories and would determine whether such a theory is right or wrong. When we look at Warren's interpretation, it seems that pleasure and pain are more earthly grounded and more simplified. In addition, utilitarianism would not be possible for Warren to accept as it provides a possibility to sacrifice the rights of the individual for the greater good. In his pamphlet, *Modern Government*, Warren paraphrased the famous paragraph from the Declaration of Independence stating that "*[e]very individual of mankind has an INALIENABLE right to Life, Liberty and the pursuit of Happiness*".[275] Moreover, the pursuit of happiness was for Warren the necessary element impelling people for mutually beneficial cooperation. Sacrificing individual happiness for any form of social good would be impossible, while Warren's entire system was built to keep the rights of individuals unviolated. Consequently, Warren seems to precede Rothbardian anti-utilitarian arguments.[276]

---

situation, and in particular in that of a functionary or set of functionaries exercising the powers of Government. The word utility does not so clearly point to the ideas of pleasure and pain as the words happiness and felicity do: nor does it lead us to the consideration of the number, of the interests affected; to the number, as being the circumstance, which contributes, in the largest proportion, to the formation of the standard here in question; the standard of right and wrong, by which alone the propriety of human conduct, in every situation, can with propriety be tried. This want of a sufficiently manifest connexion between the ideas of happiness and pleasure on the one hand, and the idea of utility on the other, I have every now and then found operating, and with but too much efficiency, as a bar to the acceptance, that might otherwise have been given, to this principle". Bentham's footnote, July 1822.

[273] Jeremy Bentham, *An Introduction to the Principles of Morals and Legislation* (Oxford: Clarendon Press, 1907) 1-2. See also Jeremy Bentham, *The Works of Jeremy Bentham, Published under the Superintendence of his Executor, John Bowring*, vol. 6 (Edinburgh: William Tait, 1838--1843) 237-238.

[274] Jeremy Bentham, *First Principles Preparatory to a Constitutional Code*, ed. P. Schofield (Oxford: Clarendon Press, 1989) 235.

[275] Josiah Warren, *Modern Government*, Folder 15: Pamphlets and Leaflets Box 1. Josiah Warren Papers, Labadie Collection, Special Collections Library, University of Michigan, my emphasis.

[276] Cf. Rothbard, *For a New Liberty*.

The reminiscences of Owen's philosophy can also be traced in the emphasis Warren puts on the pursuit of happiness. In the first constitution that established New Harmony Owen declared that "[t]he solo object of this Community will be to procure for all their Members the greatest amount of happiness, to secure it to them, and to transmit it to their children to all latest posterity".[277] This constitution appealed not only to among potential settlers but also to among public opinion.[278]

However, Warren's concept of happiness seems to resemble that of Hobbes more than its Jeffersonian or Owenite interpretations. Even though Hobbes, as many other pre-Englightenment writers, did not use the term *happiness* in his writing, he talked about felicity instead.[279] In the Hobbesian system, happiness is associated with hedonistic pleasure and passions that drive us to act. As he explains in *Leviathan*, it is the "continual progress of the desire, from one object to another; the attaining of the former, being still but the way to the latter. The cause whereof is, that the object of man's desire, is not to enjoy once only, and for one instant of time; but to assure for ever, the way of his future desire. And therefore the voluntary actions, and inclinations of all men, tend, not only to the procuring, but also to the assuring of a contented life".[280] Moreover, Hobbes is aware that there is no universal concept of happiness, and the ways individuals define and pursue their happiness differ considerably, based on a "diversity of passions, in divers men, and partly from the difference of the knowledge, or opinion each one has of the causes, which produce the effect desired".[281]

It is not surprising that one of the first pieces published by Warren was dedicated not only to the individual but also to the happiness and pursuit of happiness. "The happiness of Society must consist in the happiness of the individuals who compose it".[282] Warren defined the pursuit of happiness in a similar way to Hobbes. For both philosophers passion and inclination are the elements that drive people to take actions and determine their behavior. In Warren's theory, human beings must subdue to this passion: "Always referring to the fact, that *we are the creatures of the circumstances that surround us*, we analyze the combination of every moment,

---

[277] The Constitution of the Preliminary 2.

[278] Cf letter of George Messiger and Nathaniel Stacy to the Robert Owen, July 25th 1826, "Nathaniel Stacy Papers", box 1, folder 76. Clements Library, University of Michigan.

[279] The term is very often associated with the classical work *De legibus naturae disquisitio philosophica* from 1672 written by Richard Cumberland. The phrase "pursuit of happiness" was used for the first time in English language in its translation from 1727, cf. Richard Cumberland, J. Parkin, J. Maxwell, *A Treatise of the Laws of Nature* (Indianapolis, Ind: Liberty Fund, 2005) 570. In the original version Cumberland used the phrase *"generales causas felicitatis"*, cf. Richard Cumberland, *De Legibus Naturae Disquisitio Philosophica: In Qua Earum Forma, Summa Capita, Ordo, Promulgatio, & Obligatio E Rerum Natura Investigantur* (London: Typis E. Flesher, prostat vero apud Nathanaelem Hooke, 1672), no pagination, book V, paragraph XXXV.

[280] Thomas Hobbes, William Molesworth, Thucydides, and Homer. *The English Works of Thomas Hobbes of Malmesbury*, vol. 3 (London: J. Bohn, 1839) 87.

[281] Hobbes et al., *The English Works* 87.

[282] Warren, To the Friends of Social System (1 June 1827): 2.

and find in each some that differ from all others, but one which /is always the same, which determines every action, and which nothing can every control; this is, *my desire of happiness;* it is the first circumstance in point of importance; it is the once in comparison to which, all others sing into insignificance; it is the once which induces me to change and to modify all others to accommodate it. It is itself *omnipotent*, and I have no power whatever to control it; my only business seems to be to obey its dictates without demur; whatever stands in its way, it bids me avoid, whatever pleases it, it bids me cherish".[283] At the early stage of formulating his theory, Warren believed that our pursuit is oriented and grounded in the present time and does not take into consideration the long-term perspective: "[W]e never feel or act from any thing but *the circumstances of the present moment*".[284]

If the pursuit of happiness is the only element common to the whole mankind, it is worth analysing more deeply whether Warren treated this in a merely sensual, hedonistic way, or maybe it was closer to the notions of *eudemonia* or *beatitudo*, correlated with self-improvement and personal development. Is there an intellectual component identifying what can provide happiness to an individual? Initially, Warren's situated striving for happiness and avoiding unhappiness on the level of senses, sensual impressions and subconscious reactions. He said that "[y]our starting point is *exactly the right one*, that 'happiness, pleasure, self preservation' *is the* involuntary, instinctive, but almost unknown aim and ultimate goal of all our movements".[285] However, having described this sensual experience, Warren introduced a rational element as well. When we analyse how the process of recognition which leads to happiness is described, our mind, stimulated by words, creates notions based on earlier experiences. When we hear the word "rose", it evokes all those pleasant experiences and emotions related to the object that word indicates. When we hear the word "whiskey": "the circumstance of association presents to my mind human misery, in every shape; intoxicated men, despairing mothers, ragged starving children, pilfering, want, officers, laws, trials, convictions, dungeons and death. These are circumstances over which I have no control, and my ***desire of happiness*** bids me avoid them".[286] Thus, happiness is not a purely animalistic, sensual pleasure, and it is by no means a mere surrender to addictions. Happiness is based on the satisfaction of the senses, as they are the primary source of information about feelings and emotions. "I am informed by those senses, that some things are capable of producing unhappiness, and my desire of happiness bids me avoid or dislike them: and that some things are capable of producing happiness; and my desire of happiness bids me love and cherish them. I perceive by my senses that I have certain wants; such as protection from the elements, a supply of food, clothes, lodging; and I perceive too, that

---

[283] Warren, To the Friends of Social System (8 June 1827): 2.
[284] Warren, To the Friends of Social System (1 June 1827): 2.
[285] Josiah Warren, "Periodical Letter" 1.5 (July 1857): 66.
[286] Warren, To the Friends of the Social System (8 June 1827): 2.

I wish for change, contrast, variety; and my desire of happiness bids me find and secure them".[287]

Thus, following the initial impulse received by the human senses, the process of recognition is intellectual and rational, and demands prior knowledge which allows one to distinguish an action that helps the pursuit of one's happiness from actions providing misery. The pursuit of happiness is much more than a mere submission to the accidental passions and random needs that an individual might feel. Otherwise the individual that hears the term "whiskey" could not know all the negative side effects of addiction and alcoholism. The pursuit of happiness as defined by Warren is constant and imperishable, but also demands the unlimited right to shape the circumstances that might have an influence on the individual in his/her pursuit of happiness. Moreover, this right is universally shared by all individuals. "I desire my own happiness at every moment of my life, I wish to have at all times and in all cases, the power of 'dictating my own circumstances' in every respect, and in every point of view; and I am also anxious that all others may have the same security, in order that they may no longer feel toward me as they have done; and that I may no longer feel that fear of them which I have heretofore felt, but that by mutual *security*, we shall by sympathy enjoy each other's happiness. Perceiving that I cannot control my sensations, I wish to have power sufficient to control causes which produce them".[288]

At this point it is worth noticing that such a definition of the pursuit of happiness, understood as the total control of individuals over their lives, will have far-reaching consequences in shaping Warren's theory of sovereignty. Sovereignty must also be total and non-transferrable, otherwise people would not have complete control over their actions and would not freely pursue their happiness. However, this system has a serious flaw as Warren completely neglects unpredictable events such as natural disasters, on which the individual has no influence. Therefore, obtaining total control over one's life seems to be a utopian and unrealistic project.

The pursuit of happiness is controlling power that cannot be bound and that determines our actions. As Warren believed: "Our desire of happiness we never can control; it does at *every moment*, and for ever will, control us; therefore, for the happiness of all, let *that* be the 'dictator' for each".[289] Later on, Warren argued: "Therefore, let every one 'dictate his own circumstances,' and have the *assistance*, (not the control) of others. The organization of society is entirely *artificial*, and an invention of man".[290] Therefore, happiness and the pursuit of happiness do not provide an axiological framework, but in Warren's perspective it is essential to provide a functional background and naturally impel individuals to cooperate.

---

[287] Warren, To the Friends of the Social System (22 June 1827): 2.
[288] Warren, To the Friends of the Social System (22 June 1827): 2.
[289] Warren, To the Friends of the Social System (22 June 1827): 2.
[290] Warren, To the Friends of the Social System (22 June 1827): 2.

3.3. Warren and Proudhon

3.3.1. The earliest exposition of anarchism?

Even when we acknowledge that Proudhon was the first to use and popularise the term *anarchism*, after a careful comparison of the writings of those two philosophers we can come to the conclusion that it was actually Warren who offered a much earlier exposition of anarchism, even if he never labelled his philosophical system as the anarchist one. The earliest preserved issue of the *Peaceful Revolutionist* from April 1833 provides both anti-law and anti-government statements.[291] In addition, Schuster believed that Warren had preceded Proudhon's positive definition of anarchy.[292]

"The anarchist quest for socialism during the first half of the nineteenth century in America largely followed the idea of mutualism worked out simultaneously but independently by Josiah Warren in this country and Pierre-Joseph Proudhon in France. Primarily individualists, both Warren and Proudhon sought to eliminate inequality and economic servitude by building a strong social collectivity based upon a population of free individuals federated together in mutual support of one another without interference or control from government. In this phase of its development, anarchism was a clear reflection of Jeffersonian agrarianism".[293]

Pierre-Joseph Proudhon was the first to call himself an anarchist in a dialogue that seemed to be dressed up in a satirical costume: "What is to be the form of government in the future? I hear some of my younger readers reply: 'Why, how can you ask such a question? You are a republican.' 'A republican! Yes; but that word specifies nothing. *Res publica;* that is, the public thing. Now, whoever is interested in public affairs — no matter under what form of government—may call himself a republican. Even kings are republicans.' — 'Well! you are a democrat?' — 'No.' — 'What! you would have a monarchy.'— 'No.' —*A* constitutionalist?'—; 'God forbid!' — 'You are then an aristocrat?' — 'Not at all.' — 'You want a mixed government?' — 'Still less.' —'What are you, then?' — 'I am an anarchist.' 'Oh ! I understand you ; you speak satirically. This is a hit at the government.' — 'By no means. I have just given you my serious and well-considered profession of faith. Although a firm friend of order, I am (in the full force of the term) an anarchist. Listen to me.'"[294] This humorous dialogue from 1840 shows that since Godwin's writings that demythologised anarchy and its alleged evils, openly naming oneself an anarchist could still be highly provocative and courageous.

This is particularly true when we know that Proudhon himself was aware of this pejorative connotation when he wrote *"Anarchy,* — the absence of a master,

[291] Warren, A Brush 14.
[292] Schuster, *Native American* 93.
[293] Reichert, *Partisans* 9.
[294] Pierre-Joseph Proudhon, Benjamin R. Tucker, *The Works of P.J. Proudhon, Vol. 1, What is Property?: an Inquiry into the Principle of Right and of Government* (Princeton, Mass.: Benj. R. Tucker, 1876) 271-272.

of a sovereign,[295] — such is the form of government to which we are every day approximating, and which our accustomed habit of taking man for our rule, and his will for law, leads us to regard as the height of disorder and the expression of chaos"[296] while adding an explanation in the footnote: "The meaning ordinarily attached to the word 'anarchy' is absence of principle, absence of rule consequently, it has been regarded as synonymous with 'disorder'".[297] Later on, in the same work he argued that "Liberty is anarchy, because it does not admit the government of the will, but only the authority of the law; that is, of necessity".[298] The vision of the government Proudhon presented was limited to the hostile actions taken by the governmental officials violating individual liberty and restricting individual rights. He strongly stated that "[t]o be GOVERNED is to be at every operation, at every transaction, noted, registered, enrolled, taxed, stamped, measured, numbered, assessed, licensed, authorized, admonished, forbidden, reformed, corrected, punished. It is, under pretext of public utility, and in the name of the general interest, to be placed under contribution, trained, ransomed, exploited, monopolized, extorted, squeezed, mystified, robbed; then, at the slightest resistance, the first word of complaint, to be repressed, fined, despised, harassed, tracked, abused, clubbed, disarmed, choked, imprisoned, judged, condemned, shot, deported, sacrificed, sold, betrayed; and, to crown all, mocked, ridiculed, outraged, dishonoured. That is government; that is its justice; that is its morality".[299] It is clear from this passage that Proudhon did not find any positive aspect of being governed.

The fundamental element of Proudhon's social thought was his libertarian idealism which led him to hope that in the future humans would realise the social strengths they are capable of by nature in giving human's imagination free reign. "Man is by nature a sinner,—that is, not essentially ill-doing, but rather ill-done,— and it is his destiny to perpetually re-create his ideal in himself"[300], Proudhon wrote in his *Solution du problème social* of the ideal republic as *a positive anarchy*. "It is neither liberty, subordinated to order, as in a constitutional monarchy, nor liberty in presenting order. It is reciprocal liberty and not limited liberty; liberty is not the daughter but the mother of order".[301]

---

[295] "The meaning ordinarily attached to the word 'anarchy' is absence of principle, absence of rule; consequently, it has been regarded as synonymous with 'disorder'". – the Proudhon's original footnote.

[296] Proudhon, and Tucker, *The Works* (1876) 271-272.

[297] Proudhon, and Tucker, *The Works* (1876) 277.

[298] Proudhon, and Tucker, *The Works* (1876) 281.

[299] Pierre Joseph Proudhon, *General Idea of Revolution in the Nineteenth Century*, J.B. Robinson Ed. (London, Freedom Press 1923) 294.

[300] Pierre Joseph Proudhon, Benjamin R Tucker, *System of Economical Contradictions; Or, the Philosophy of Misery, Transl. from the French by B.r. Tucker. Vol. I.* (Boston: Tucker, 1888) 434.

[301] Proudhon, P.-J, Charles A. Dana, William B. Greene, and Henry Cohen *Proudhon's Solution of the Social Problem.* (New York: Vanguard Press, 1927) 45; G. D. H. Cole, *A History of Socialist Thought: Vol. 1. Socialist Thought. the Forerunners 1789-1850* (London: Macmillan, 1953) 202.

As Carter observed, "[i]t is this myth-making conception of representation, and the related idea of sovereignty, that Proudhon attacked, arguing that government by the grace of the people was replacing government by the grace of God, and the idol of the people being enthroned in place of the idol of the king. Moreover, said Proudhon, the supposed delegate of the sovereign people will always become the master. Whether parliamentary assemblies usurp, through the ritual of elections, the interpretation of the general will, or a dictator usurps it from parliament through the magic of a plebiscite, the concept of 'sovereign will' provides a justification for centralized power and for sweeping aside all barriers to the exercise of this power".[302]

The question is which of those two thinkers presented a system of no imposed authority that permitted individuals to fully exercise their liberty. Carter refers to Colin Ward, who pointed out four elements that are essential for any anarchist system:

1) voluntary,
2) functional,
3) temporary, and
4) small

"They should be voluntary for obvious reasons. There is no point in our advocating individual freedom and responsibility if we are going to advocate organisations for which membership is mandatory. They should be functional and temporary precisely because permanence is one of those factors which harden the arteries of an organisation, giving it a vested interest in its own survival, in serving the interests of office-holders rather than its function. They should be small precisely because in small face-to-face groups, the bureaucratising and hierarchical tendencies inherent in organisations have least opportunity to develop".[303]

When we define anarchism by those four constructive elements, there is no doubts that Warren was as much an anarchist as Proudhon was. Also, both of them had a similar kind of anarchism in mind. As Carter pointed out, "[t]he type of anarchism developed by Pierre-Joseph Proudhon, who first adopted the title 'anarchist', idealized the sturdy independence of the small peasant proprietor or skilled craftsman, and proposed a type of co-operative organization appropriate to the economic needs of this kind of community and to a society of independent equals".[304] However, if we define *an-arche* as the ideal form of order based on the association of small, independent peasant proprietors and skilled craftsmen, we need to admit that such an ideal had been developed and expressed prior to Proudhon.

---

[302] April Carter, *The Political Theory of Anarchism* (London: Routledge and K. Paul, 1971) 51.

[303] Collin Ward, "The organisation of Anarchy," *Patterns of Anarchy – A Collection of Writings on the Anarchist Tradition*, ed. Leonard I. Krimerman and Lewis Perry (Garden City, NY: Anchor Books, 1966) 386.

[304] Carter, *The Political Theory* 2.

This ideal was typical for the early American Jeffersonian tradition and then carried out and hyperbolised by Warren in the late 1820s and early 1830s. Warren's philosophical system was fully developed and communicated to the public in 1846 when he published *Equitable Commerce*. Regardless whether we assume that Warren's system originated in the late 1820s or even as late as in 1846, his ideas had been published undisputedly before Proudhon's *What is Property*.[305] Therefore, Schuster even called Warren "American Proudhon".[306] Granting Warren the same status as Proudhon was also done in the nineteenth century when George Holyoake reprinted in 1958 Edmund Burke's *A Vindication of Natural Society: A View of the Miseries and Evils Arising to Mankind* under the title of *The Inherent Evils of all State Governments Demonstrated*. In the Appendix (probably written by A.C. Cuddon), the author referred, without mentioning his name, to Pierre-Joseph Proudhon and to Josiah Warren as the continuators of Burke's idea "that *State* governments will never give real freedom to their subjects".[307]

Rejecting labels and all *-isms*, Warren could not have advocated for anarchism just as he did not advocate for individualism. He demanded, however, that individual liberty be unrestrained by the government in the same manner as he demanded unrestrained individuality and separation of persons. Therefore, in the case of Warren it is evident that his unlabelled individualism is parallel to his unlabelled anarchism. Since the very beginning, liberty and freedom were essential for Warren. He wrote "LIBERTY is the vital principle of human happiness; and human nature seeks its *liberty* as the magnet seeks the north, or as water seeks its level; and society can never know peace until its members know LIBERTY; but it can never be realized under any organization of society now known to us, nor can it ever be attained upon any of the theories upon which societies are now acting"![308] Such ideas, redundantly paraphrased, recurred in Warren's writing, making the author undoubtedly the first American champion of anarchy.

Warren was aware that none of the political regimes that had ever existed provided unlimited individual liberty: "Liberty is violated, and always has been violated, in every organization of society of which I have any knowledge, either ancient or modern".[309] What Warren proposed was the end of the regimes in

---

[305] Warren's *Equitable Commerce* from 1846 has the vast passages that are either dated as written in 1840 or that can be identified as identical with passages from the Notebook D, dated also 1840. It is highly impossible that Warren had access to Proudhon's book immediately after it had been published in France. There is no doubt that Warren and Proudhon built their system independently, and that Warren preceded Proudhon.

[306] Schuster *Native American* 92.

[307] Edmund Burke, *The Inherent Evils of All State Governments Demonstrated: Being a Reprint of Edmund Burke's Celebrated Essay, Entitled "a Vindication of Natural Society", with Notes and an Appendix, Briefly Enunciating the Principles Through Which "Natural Society" May Be Gradually Realized.* (London: Holyoake, 1858) 58-60.

[308] Warren, *Practical Details* (1852) 12.

[309] Warren, *Practical Details* (1852) 76.

which *"Liberty defined and limited by others [was] slavery.* That every one has an inalienable right to define this and all other words for himself or herself, and therefore, that no one has any right to define them for others".[310] It is evident that such unlimited liberty is possible only with the lack of artificial *arche* imposed upon individuals by external factors. Bowman N. Hall, likewise, interpreted Warren's individualism as a form of anarchism, believing that "[i]n Warren's writings, the importance of individual sovereignty stood out, for the individual is the *sine qua* non of anarchisms. Warren thus is not only America's first anarchist, and a non-violent and individualistic one at that, but one who began propagandizing his ideas some sixty years before the Chicago Haymarket Affair".[311]

Therefore, if we defined anarchism as William Bailie did in the early twentieth century as the philosophy that "would allow the individual to find out for himself what was best, without restraint or coercion (...) [and] maintain complete equality of rights and opportunities, leaving it to each person, singly or in association with others, to work out his own destiny in accordance with his capacities, temperament and desires",[312] there is no doubt that Warren should be perceived as the first American anarchist.

3.3.2. The role of private property

An analysis of Proudhon's ideas about property is rather difficult due to Proudhon's character. Woodcock quoted in his introduction to Proudhon's biography the confession that Proudhon made: "I distrust an author who pretends to be consistent with himself after an interval of twenty-five years".[313] Woodcock, therefore, called Proudhon "a man of paradoxes", a man who took pride in inconsistency. Cole, describing Proudhon, stated that "[h]e was never a system--maker, and was usually more at home in criticism than in construction".[314] This is evident when we attempt to search in Proudhon's writing for a coherent system of ideas regarding property and particularly the notion of private property. There have been various interpretations of Proudhon's theory of property[315] but

---

[310] Warren, *Equitable Commerce*, 1846, 72.

[311] N. H. Bowman N. "The Economic Ideas of Josiah Warren, First American Anarchist," *History of Political Economy*. 6.1 (1974): 107.

[312] Bailie, *Josiah Warren* xxiv-xxv.

[313] George Woodcock, *Pierre-Joseph Proudhon: A Biography* (Montréal: Black Rose Books, 1987) XIII.

[314] Cole, *A history vol. 1* 201.

[315] Among the most often quoted is George Woodcock, *Pierre-Joseph*; K. Steven Vincent, *Pierre-Joseph Proudhon and the Rise of French Republican Socialism* (Oxford: Oxford University Press, 1984); Charles A. Dana, *Proudhon and his Bank of People* (New York: B.R.Tucker, 1896). Also Robert Hoffman's *Revolutionary Justice: The Social and Political Theory of P.J. Proudhon* (Urbana, Ill: University of Illinois, 1972) and K. Steven Vincent's *Pierre-Joseph Proudhon and the Rise of French Republican Socialism* (New York: Oxford University Press, 1984) are iconic interpretations. Recently the most interesting attempts to revive Proudhon's philosophy were taken by Shawn P. Wilburn and Iain McKay. There is also a vast body of non-English literature, with the most relevant written

undoubtedly what brought him enormous fame was his well-known phrase that "Property is theft". Even though it has been disputed that he was the person who coined it.[316] Hoffman pointed out the provocative nature of Proudhon's writings.[317] Undoubtedly, the readers' attention was caught not only by Proudhon's rhetorical phrases but mainly by the fact that he tried to challenge the institution that had been so deeply rooted in society – the institution that in Hoffman's opinion was "in a broad sense far more sacred than the Catholic Church".[318]

However, Proudhon's theory of property is more complex than this slogan. In *What is Property* Proudhon compiled a list of ten reasons why property is impossible, while he defined it as "the Right of Increase claimed by the Proprietor over any thing which he has stamped as his own:

1) Property is Impossible, because it demands Something for Nothing
2) Property is Impossible, because, wherever it exists, Production costs more than it is worth
3) Property is Impossible, because, with a given Capital, Production is proportional to Labor, not to Property
4) Property is Impossible, because it is Homicide
5) Property is Impossible, because, if it exists, Society devours itself
6) Property is Impossible, because it is the Mother of Tyranny
7) Property is Impossible, because, in consuming its Receipts, it loses them ; in hoarding them, it nullifies them ; and, in using them as Capital, it turns them against Production

---

in French: Aimé Berthod, *P.J. Proudhon Et La Propriété: Un Socialisme Pour Les Paysans.* (Paris: V. Giard & E. Brière, 1910) and Jules L. Puech, *Le Proudhonisme Dans L'association Internationale Des Travailleurs* (Paris: F. Alcan, 1907). In the German language: K. Diehl, *P. J. Proudhon, seine Lehre und seine Leben*, 3 vol. (Jena: Fisher, 1888-1890-1896); Max Nettlau *Geschite die anarchie* vol. 1-3 (Berlin: Asy-Verlag, 1925-1931). In Italian: Giampietro D. Berti, *La Dimensione Libertaria Di Pierre-Joseph Proudhon* (Roma: Città Nuova, 1982).

[316] According to W. Ducket and Henrie de Lubac, the original author of the saying *property is theft* was Brissot de Warville, cf. William Duckett, *Dictionnaire de la conversation et de la lecture: Inventaire raisonne des notions generales les plus indispensables a tous, par une societe de savants et de gens de lettres, sous la dir.de M.W.Duckett. 2e ed.corr.et augm.de plusieurs milliers d'articles d'actualite* (Paris: Didot, 1863) 138; Henri de Lubac, R. E. Scantlebury, *The un-Marxian Socialist: A Study of Proudhon* (New York: Sheed & Ward, 1948) 174). Lubac quotes Brissot de Warville "Exclusive property is a theft in nature. The theft, in the nature state, is the rich man". However, in Warville's work *Recherche sur le droit de propriété et le vol* from 1782 the quote is quite different, and the exact passage is: "Exclusive property is a true crime against the nature" (Car cette propriété exclusive est un crime véritable dans la nature)" (W. J.-P. Brissot, *Recherches philosophiques sur le droit de propriété: Considéré dans la nature ; pour servir de premier chapître à la Théorie des loix de M. Linguet.* (Chartres, 1780): 42. Also Robert Graham confirmed that "The claim that Proudhon took this phrase from the Girondin, J.P. Brissot de Warville, repeated by Marx after his break with Proudhon, has been decisively refuted by Robert L. Hoffman. Cf. Hoffman, *Revolutionary Justice* 46–48". Cf. Robert Graham, "The General Idea of Proudhon's Revolution", http://dwardmac.pitzer. edu/Anarchist_Archives/proudhon/grahamproudhon.html (accessed 04.22.2015).

[317] Hoffman, *Revolutionary Justice of Proudhon* 40.

[318] Hoffman, *Revolutionary Justice* 40.

8) Property is Impossible, because its Power of Accumulation is infinite, and is exercised only over Finite Quantities.

9) Property is Impossible, because it is powerless against Property

10) Property is Impossible, because it is the Negation of Equality".[319]

   Proudhon perceived property as a result of the unfinished revolutions of 1789 and 1830, when the notion received its distorted meaning. He claimed that "[t]hese, then, are the three fundamental principles of modern society, established one after another by the movements of 1789 and 1830: 1. *Sovereignty of the human will*; in short, despotism. 2. *Inequality of wealth and rank*. 3· *Property* above JUSTICE, always invoked as the guardian angel of sovereigns, nobles, and proprietors".[320] Then his aim was to "ascertain whether the ideas of despotism, civil inequality, and property, are in harmony with the primitive notion of justice, and necessarily follow from it – assuming various forms according to the condition, position, and relation of persons; or whether they are not rather the illegitimate result of a confusion of different things, a fatal association of ideas. And since justice deals especially with the questions of government, the condition of persons, and the possession of things, we must ascertain under what conditions, judging by universal opinion and the progress of the human mind, government is just, the condition of citizens is just, and the possession of things is just".[321] Proudhon also returned to this concept in the *Letter to Considerant*, trying to provide a clearer explanation of his notion of property while refuting the Fourierist arguments.[322] He expressed his dissatisfaction with the existing interpretation of property arguing that "[t]he second effect of property is despotism. Now, since despotism is inseparably connected with the idea of legitimate authority, in explaining the natural causes of the first, the principle of the second will appear".[323] Also Iain McKay noticed that "Proudhon's critique rested on two key concepts. Firstly, property allowed the owner to exploit its user ('property is theft'). Secondly, that property created authoritarian and oppressive social relationships between the two ('property is despotism'). These are interrelated, as it is the relations of oppression that property creates which allows exploitation to happen and the appropriation of our common heritage by the few gives the rest little alternative but to agree to such domination and let the owner appropriate the fruits of their labour".[324]

---

[319] Proudhon, and Tucker, *The Works* (1876) vi-vii.

[320] Proudhon, and Tucker, *The Works* (1876) 37.

[321] Proudhon, and Tucker, *The Works*(1876) 37.

[322] Pierre-Joseph Proudhon, M. Considerant, *Avertissement aux propriétaires, ou, Lettre à M. Considérant, rédacteur de la Phalange, sur une défense de la propriété* (Paris: Garnier, 1848) 58-72.

[323] Proudhon, Tucker, *The Works* (1876), 271.

[324] Pierre-Joseph Proudhon, and Iain McKay, *Property Is Theft!: A Pierre-Joseph Proudhon Anthology* (Baltimore: AK Press, 2011) 6.

Upon closer examination of the notion of Proudhonian property, it becomes evident that Proudhon did not demand to abolish it but desired to make it just. The notion of justice will be, besides the notion of property, another core element of Proudhon's system. Accordingly, Georgiï V. Plekhanov, in his iconic *Anarchism and Socialism*, observed that for Proudhon "[l]abour is the source and the measure of the *value* of commodities. But is the *price* of commodities always determined by their value? Do not prices continually vary according to the rarity or abundance of these commodities? The value of a commodity and its price are two different things; and this is the misfortune, the great misfortune of all of us poor, honest folk, who only want justice, and only ask for our own. To solve the social question, therefore we must put a stop to the *arbitrariness of prices*, and to the anomaly of value (Proudhon's own expressions). And in order to do this we must 'constitute' value; *i.e.*, see that every producer shall always, in exchange for his commodity, receive exactly what it costs. Then will private property not only cease to be theft, it will become the most adequate expression of justice. To constitute value is to constitute small private property, and small private property once constituted, everything will be justice and happiness in a world now so full of misery and injustice".[325] Proudhon appeared to be quite close to the solution offered by Warren, who was also seeking to avoid the arbitrariness of prices, and to void the *anomaly of value*, but Warren achieved both those aims by setting the cost of production as the limit of price.

However, the solution that Proudhon offered in terms of economic theories was not designed for a large scale. As Cole pointed out, "Proudhon always thought of society and of its problems mainly in terms of small-scale economic activity and of small social groups. He had indeed in mind mainly peasant families cultivating their small farms, or individual craftsmen carrying on small-scale production, and he regarded the tendency towards large-scale industrial organization as mainly a result of economic inequality and wrong social conditions".[326] In this aspect, Warren and Proudhon's economic propositions reveal similarities; it is hard to imagine that Warren's project might be adapted on a large scale, even though he claimed that it was universally applicable. Warren's approach to private property is quite evident, and his conclusion to not transfer individual sovereignty to other collective bodies is mainly grounded in the conviction that the absolute right over his/her body and property is irreconcilable with any external interference. Warren might have condemned "social canibalism" and the distribution of surplus income, but it did not prevent him from being a strong advocate of the individual right for private property.

Also, for Warren, the only possibility for the full protection of private property would be a complete annihilation of the government. As Warren stated, "[i]t is impossible for any one who can read the history of governments, and the operations

---

[325] Georgiï V. Plekhanov, *Anarchism and Socialism* (Chicago: C.H. Kerr & Co., 1909) 66-67.
[326] Cole, *A History vol. 1* 210.

of laws to feel secure in person or property under any form of government, or any code of laws whatever. They invade the private household, they [impertinently] meddle with, and in their blind and besotted wantonness, presume to regulate the most sacred individual feelings. No feelings of security, no happiness".[327]

3.3.3. Anarchist economy – just reward for labour – the quest for equality

Warren and Proudhon established the foundations of anarchist economy. They both tried, in a quest for a more equitable reward for labour, to transform the property system into the system that would be more just. As Gerard Runkle observed, "Josiah Warren, the first significant American anarchist, developed similar ideas in apparent ignorance of Proudhon's work. The American mutualists and individualists who followed – John Beverley Robinson, Benjamin R. Tucker, and Stephen Pearl Andrews – built on the work of Warren or Proudhon, or both".[328] Proudhon was aware of inequalities, and he proposed a complex system of altering economic relations that might offer a remedy and improve not only the living conditions of the workers but create a just system of government. Shin Yung Lu mentioned Proudhon's multiple economic propositions, among them two different kinds of reforms: industrial and commercial. The industrial reform would be built on the following three elements:

"a. The right to labor guaranteed to everyone.

b. The division of labor.

c. The suppression of the distinction between labor and capital by the equalizing of wage and product".[329]

On the other hand, the commercial reform would consist of the three elements:

"a. The organization of credit and exchange, on the basis of reciprocity.

b. The abolition of the system of purchase and sale by fixing in advance the exact price of each commodity by the producer-consumers".[330]

The right to labour was explicitly guaranteed by Proudhon, who could not imagine a situation of unemployment believing that "[i]ntelligence and natural genius have been distributed by Nature so economically, and yet so liberally, that in society there is no danger of either a surplus or a scarcity of special talents; and that each laborer, by devoting himself to his function, may always attain to the degree of proficiency necessary to enable him to benefit by the labors and discoveries of his fellows".[331] Therefore, the right to labour became an essential

---

[327] Warren, *Equitable Commerce* (1846) 19-20.

[328] Gerald Runkle, *Anarchism, Old and New* (New York: Delacorte Press, 1972) 80.

[329] S. Y. Lu, *The Political Theories of P.J. Proudhon* (New York: M.R. Gray, 1922) 58.

[330] Lu, *The Political* 58.

[331] Pierre-Joseph Proudhon, *What is Property?: An Inquiry into the Principle of Right and of Government* (Princeton, Mass.: Benj. R. Tucker, 1876) 239.

element of Proudhon's public economy and jurisprudence.[332] He also believed in the division of labour,[333] while in Warren's economy we can identify the unspoken call for flexibility and the quick apprenticeship to any new profession. This could be a flash of Warren's genius and his many skills and abilities.

As Cole observed, the French Co-operative school as well as Louis Blanc's theory, as in Fourier's and as in Owen's proposition, the practical activities of society would be "in the hands of '*les associations*'. The self-governing association was to be the characteristic and omnipresent agent of the citizens in the collective conduct of their affairs. (...). 'The State' was to be transformed into an expression of the true power in modern society — *les producteurs*. (...) Proudhon was suspicious of the power element in associations, as well as of the State — suspicious of every kind of organisation that limited the freedom of the individual beyond what was absolutely necessary to ensure its ' reciprocal' character — that is, its *not* refusing equal freedom to other men. In Proudhon's thought the key position was held, not by ' association', but by the family".[334] Furthermore, "The family and the individual were never separated in his mind: he thought of them as one and the same".[335] For Warren, however, even the family would be too oppressive form of collectivisation, and the individual principle would demand the dissolving of all interests – even within the family unit.

"The essence of 'contract', according to Proudhon, is that each man should be free to make what arrangements he pleases with other men under conditions which will ensure that all are in a position to bargain freely and that no monopoly of power or wealth upsets the fairness of the bargain. 'Contract', for Proudhon, was the essentially free commitment of the responsible individual, and therefore the necessary mode of action for men living in a free society. He carried this conception of 'contract' so far as to mistrust all forms of association which require men to give up direct action in their individual capacities in favour of action through any sort of collective or representative agency which takes away their personal responsibility".[336]

Proudhon did not call for the abolition of inequality but for the abolition of injustice. Imposed equality would be destructive and would undermine incentives to work. "What was needed was the abolition, not of inequality, but of injustice — that is, of inequalities resting not on unequal labours, but on privilege and monopoly. Every individual, every family, should receive the full fruit of their labours in accordance with the principle of fair exchange. It was this principle that

---

[332] "Equality of conditions is a natural law upon which public economy and jurisprudence are based. The right to labor, and the principle of equal distribution of wealth, cannot give way to the anxieties of power". Proudhon, *What is property?* 248.

[333] Pierre-Joseph Proudhon and John B. Robinson, *General Idea of the Revolution in the Nineteenth Century* (New York: Haskell House Publishers, 1969) 215-224.

[334] Cole, *A History vol. 1* 204-205.

[335] Cole, *A History vol. 1* 205.

[336] Cole, *A History vol. 1* 210.

all Proudhon's economic proposals were intended to further and to protect. On this he founded his conception of 'gratuitous credit', of 'mutuality', and of a society resting on 'free contracts' between its members. 'It is the business of the State only to pronounce on the justice of economic relationships, not to determine the manifestations of freedom.' Thus Proudhon expressed himself in his *Solution of the Social Problem*, written in 1848. In many of his books he refused to assign to 'the State' even this limited role; but in this work he was endeavouring to formulate an immediate programme for the new Government set up by the February Revolution. In the same passage he declared against Louis Blanc's demand for the 'organisation of labour'. It is not the *organisation of labour* that we need at this moment. The organisation of labour is the proper object of individual freedom. He who works hard gains much. The State has nothing further to say, in this matter, to the workers. What we need, what I call for in the name of all workers, is reciprocity, equity in exchange, the *organisation of credit*'."[337]

Proudhon advocated the opening of a Credit Bank – an independent institution separate from the state, making interest-free advances of capital through subsidiary branches, to ensure means of labour to each producer or workers' organisation and to ensure to each producer the full product of his labour. Products would be exchanged at cost value by means of labour checks based on the labour-time theory of value associated with Robert Owen and the Ricardian socialists.[338] As we know, Warren's practice preceded Proudhon's proposition.[339]

Warren did not think about a nationwide mutual banking system, but rather a small labour for labour exchange, embedded in the reality of locality and provincial environment. Additionally, he openly admitted that "we want a circulating medium that is a definite representative of a definite quantity of property, and nothing but a representative; so that when we cannot make direct equivalent exchanges of property, we can supply the deficiency with its definite representative, which will stand in its place. And this should not have any reference to the value of the property, but only to its COST, so that if I get a bushel of wheat of you, I give you the representative of shoe-making, with which you should be able to obtain from the shoemaker as much labor as you bestowed on the wheat – cost for cost in equivalent quantities".[340] The *labour note*, or, as other writers called it later, the *labour dollar*, proposed by Warren, was in his opinion the only remedy for pecuniary relations.

What is the most important when we think about Warren's economy is the fact that it was tested in practice. As Carter pointed out, "more formative influence on later American anarchism was Josiah Warren's attempt to put individualist anarchism into practice, through experimental co-operatives, in the 1830s and

[337] Cole, *A History vol. 1* 206.
[338] Pierre Joseph Proudhon, *Résumé de la question sociale, banque d'échange* (Paris : Garnier, 1849) 41-53.
[339] Schuster, *Native Anarchism* 103.
[340] Warren, *Equitable Commerce* (1852): 67.

1840s. Warren propagated ideas on economic organization and private property not unlike those Proudhon was independently putting forward in France"[341] The longevity of Warren's economic experiments such as *Time Stores* in Cincinnati and New Harmony, the economy based on the *cost the limit of price* principle in Tuscarawa, Utopia and Modern Times are strong proofs that in small agrarian and artisan communities such an economic system was not only plausible, but highly profitable for individuals.

---

[341] Carter, *The Political Theory* 7-8.

INSTEAD OF CONCLUSION

> Governments can be dispensed with, independence can not be if a just society was the final objective.
>
> Warren, *Letter To H.R., Texas*, "Word", vol. 1, no. 3, July 1872, 1.

As Shively wrote, "Every man is an enigma, and Warren is no exception. In outer appearance he did not seem extraordinary. Short, stout, strong, he might well have been a simply a carpenter. Only his blue eyes projecting their brightness from behind bushy eyebrows revealed the mystery within. In demeanor, he was not flighty, for he moved slowly and deliberately; yet there was a restlessness in his movements which did not fit with his otherwise placid features. As from without, so from within this man showed two contradictory attributes: the placid, scientific, impersonal, exact perfectionist; and the adventurous, roving, kind, generous, romantic reformer".[342]

Whether we can validate the claim about real popularity of Warren's *Time Store* or not, his economic experiment was one of the most interesting economic theories of the nineteenth century. Despite the lack of unanimity among scholars on whether it was Warren or Owen who first invented the labour notes, there is no doubt that Warren was the first one who had put this idea into practice and popularised it in the United States and Great Britain. *Time Stores* were seedbed for contemporary time-banking or barter exchange of goods that we have been able to observe in many countries, recently in Greece after the crisis.

"This modern aspect of anarchism suggests that attention be paid to its precursors and to the family of anarchistic doctrines as they have come forth during a hundred and fifty years. The term is here employed in its original sense of rejection or weakening of the coercive power of government as well as its instruments of politics and legislation, in opposition to the socialistic doctrines of political action and increased power of the State controlled by the labour vote. In this sense the germs of anarchistic doctrine are found wherever we find a demand for the abolition of property titles, vested rights, or regulation by law, leaving individuals to the 'free' exercise of their 'natural rights,' or leaving groups of individuals to the 'free' exercise of whatever powers they have of combination,

---

[342] Shively, *A Remarkable American* 93.

cooperation, or even coercion. It is a fundamental contradiction of anarchism that sooner or later its adherents are forced to resort to politics and state action in order to abolish state action; but in such case the consistency of the doctrine is maintained by weakening the power of the State at the point where it interferes with the private interests of its adherents, as against the socialistic effort to strengthen the power of the state against opposing classes. In this sense, the anarchistic doctrine, appearing in its mildest form as 'free trade', and, by going deeper in the rejection of politics, of titles to property, of vested rights or state regulation, has taken the form of free banking', "free land', 'free capital', 'greenbackism', voluntary co-operation, boycotting, exemption of unions from conspiracy laws, and finally syndicalism. In one direction it has run off to the individualistic anarchism of Warren in the thirties, Andrews in the fifties, Tucker in the eighties; in another to the communistic or cooperative anarchism of Fourier, Brisbane, Greeley, Weitling of the thirties and forties and the labour unions of the sixties and seventies; while in still another direction it has taken the coercive form of the boycott, and the strike of 'conservative' unionism, going to the violent extreme of syndicalism, foreshadowed by Bakunin, practiced by the Chicago anarchists, and exalted into a philosophy by the French unions, and the Industrial Workers of the World".[343]

But Warren's economic theory offers much more than the idea of *Time Store*. It is a heroic attempt to create a combination of equality, individual liberty and private property. In Warren's system, individuals voluntarily decline extra income believing that social relations should be based on cooperation, not on the competition and "social cannibalism". At the same time, individuals sustain their complete and total sovereignty over their persons and their property. Therefore, Mill's claim that "Mr. Warren is remarkable American" is well-grounded. Moreover, a closer examination of Warren's intellectual framework also reveals the American flavour of his philosophy that was marked and shaped by the depressions of 1819 and 1837, one was the first attempt to face the modern capitalism and the changes of the market. At the same time, Warren's activities represent yet another attempt to fulfil the American utopian dream, that is, in Warren's case, the dream to pursue the more equitable society.

As Ezra Heywood observed, Warren's thought was "really only a new assertion of the ideas of self-rule and self-support which Jefferson put into the Declaration of 1776; which suggested the doctrines of "Cost the limit of Price" and "Individual Sovereignty" proclaimed by Josiah Warren from New Harmony, Indiana, in 1830; which inspired Adam Smith's Wealth of Nations a hundred years ago; which Proudhon announced from Paris in 1840; and which appear in the last utterance of John Stuart Mill".[344]

---

[343] Commons et al., *History of Labour* (1921) 16-17.

[344] Ezra H. Heywood, *The Great Strike: Its Relations to Labour, Property, and Government. Suggested by the Memorable Events which, Originating in the Tyrannous Extortion of Railway Masters, and the Execution of Eleven Labour Reformers, Called "Mollie Maguires," June 21, 1877, Culminated in Burning the Corporation Property, in Pittsburg, July 22, Following* (Princeton, Mass.: Co-operative Publishing Co., 1878) 19. (this pamphlet is reprinted from the Radical Review).

Although Warren never used the term *anarchism*, nor had he ever defined himself as an anarchist, his philosophical framework was heavily marked by the notions of:

* radical and uncompromised love of the individualism,
* conviction about superiority of any form of organization based on individual principles,
* faith that every individual is the sovereign of himself or herself and has total power to rule his or her life,
* conviction that such a power cannot be transferred or delegated under any circumstances,
* strong opposition to any form of limitation of the individual absolute right to act according to his or her wishes as long as they do not interfere with the similar rights ascribed to others.

All those elements allow to state firmly not only that Warren was the father of American anarchism and the first American anarchist, but also that many of his ideas were formed and disseminated earlier than the ideas of Proudhon. Consequently, it is possible to claim that Warren was not only the first American anarchist, but the first anarchist ever. Warren's anarchism is obvious throughout his writings. "What constitutes liberty? Who shall decide? If governments decide, then there is no liberty for the governed? Each cannot decide at his own *cost* in any national or other combination. *Liberty, therefore, cannot exist* until all combinations and united interests are dissolved back again into INDIVIDUALITIES.(...) It is frequently remarked that these principles, carried out, 'would render all laws unnecessary'".[345]

From the moment of his departure from New Harmony until his very last breath, Warren objected to forming any kind of government and any authority that would limit the individuality and individual sovereignty. "I venture the assertion that the establishing of such [governing] powers has been the greatest error of mankind, and that society will never enjoy peace or security until it has done with these barbarisms and acknowledges the *'inalienable'* right of every individual to the sovereignty of their own person, time and property".[346] Warren's ideal system was based on "no organization, no indefinite delegated power, no 'constitution', no 'laws', nor 'bye-laws', 'rules' or 'regulation' but such as each individual makes for himself and his own business. No officers, no priests, nor prophets have been resorted to – nothing of either kind has been in demand".[347]

One of the clearest declarations of his anarchist convictions can be found in his *True Civilization*, where he confessed: "Admitting this indestructible right of Sovereignty in *every Individual, at all times and in all conditions*, one will not attempt to *govern* (but only guide or lead) another; but we shall trust to principle or *purpose* for a general and voluntary coincidence and co-operation. Military

---

[345] Warren, and Andrews, *Practical Details* 81-82.
[346] Warren, *The Peaceful Revolutionist* 5 Apr. 1833: 15.
[347] Warren, *The Peaceful Revolutionist*, May 1848.

officers will then become directors or leaders,-- *not 'commanders,'*-- obedience will be all the more prompt because it is rendered for *an object*-- the greatest that can inspire human action, RESISTANCE TO ALL ATTEMPTS AT OFFENSIVE AND UNNECESSARY GOVERNING OR ENCROACHMENTS upon ANY persons or property whatsoever, as the great guarantee for the security of each and every individual. Then every Man, Woman, and Child in the world is interested in acting for and with such a government"![348] In another passage he observed that "[r]ulers claim a right to rise above and control the individual, his labor, his trade, his time, and his property against his own judgment and inclination, while security of person and property CANNOT CONSIST IN ANY THING LESS THAN HAVING THE SUPREME GOVERNMENT OF HIMSELF, AND ALL HIS OWN INTERESTS; therefore, security cannot exist under any government whatever".[349]

Despite all the evidence, why is it sometimes not so obvious to perceive Warren as the first anarchist? On the one hand, the cliché that anarchists are bomb throwers and not peaceful intellectuals is partially to blame. On the other hand, in America, anarchism is associated with the working class and European migrants. As Douthy observed, "[t]here was apparently little association between the native individualist anarchists of the Warren school and the immigrant anarchists-German, Italian, Russian, and others- who flooded into the country beginning about 1880".[350] Theses anarchists had little in common with Warren, who represented the best Bostonian intellectual tradition. Even Ezra Heywood emphasised in 1878 that Warren's opponents who labelled this system "Compulsory 'communism' (...) of foreign origin" were mistaken because "[i]t is really only a new assertion of the ideas of self-rule and self-support of which Jefferson put into the Declaration of 1776; which suggested the doctrines of 'Cost the limit of Price' and 'Individual Sovereignty' proclaimed by Josiah Warren from New Harmony, Indiana, in 1830; which inspired Adam Smith's Wealth of Nations a hundred years ago (...) and which appear in the last utterance of John Stuart Mill".[351]

Another reason why it has been difficult to classify Warren as an anarchist is his strong hostility against being classified – quite opposite to the Proudhon's self-proclamation labelling himself as an anarchist. First of all and above all, Warren was an individualist. In his *Periodical Letter*, he wrote: "*Think for instance of seeing yourself classed as one of the rank and file of a new sect, of Clan or ism, (...) This is most particularly odious to one who understand his right of Individuality*".[352] Thus, being labelled as an anarchist would be repulsive to him, not because he detested anarchy, but because for such a passionate lover of individuality any form of categorisation would be insulting.

---

[348] Warren, *True Civilization* (1863) 22.
[349] Warren, *Equitable Commerce* (1846) 21.
[350] H. M. Douty, "The Word and the Deed-Anarchism Revisited," *Monthly Labour Review* 89.1 (Jan. 1966): 17.
[351] Heywood, *The Great Strike* 19.
[352] Josiah Warren, „Periodical Letter" 1.5 (Dec. 1854): 77.

BIOGRAPHICAL NOTE[353]

My father was born In Boston, Mass. in 1798. He and his brother George joined the „Old Boston Brigade Band" while very young. In 1821 my father came west, settled in Cincinnati and followed the profession of music for some time.

The same year, he invented a lamp for burning lard, as the only artificial light then used was the tallow candle. As tallow was twenty-five cents a pound, and lard only three cents, this invention was a revelation, this being before lard oil was known. The patent documents for the lard lamp were signed by President John Quincy Adams. The patents on the printing presses invented by my father were Issued under the signature of Andrew Jackson, and B.P. Butler, in 1855. The lard lamp Invention developed into a large lamp manufactory located in Cincinnati, where the lamp business was carried on for years.

But when Robert Owen Community was started at New Harmony, Indiana my father became interested in the Owen movement. He sold out the lamp factory and moved to New Harmony, Indiana. „The citizens of the Owen Community were of the most elegant, well educated and refined class of people", but my father soon saw that connected interests, in ownership of property annihilated Individual interests, and also destroyed individual responsibility for short-comings. Very soon this s orifice of personal liberty to transact business as he chose, proved the fallacy of the communistic scheme.

Mr. Owen was a man of pure, liberal and honest motives, and while scores of pages have been devoted to his abuse, not a person who wrote this abuse ever knew what purity was compared with that of Robert Owen and his family of four sons – Robert Dale, Williams, David and Richard.

Seeing the great mistake of the connected Interest system, ray father left New Harmony for Cincinnati, and followed again the musical profession, at the same time musing over the problem of "true civilization" and "labour for labour" doctrine. In those days to print a paper was an expensive undertaking and, as my father had no money, the question was how to get his ideas before the people.

---

[353] This is the transcript of the biographical notes left by George Warren describing the life of his father. There is no manuscript and the existing version has been typed, probably by Agnes Inglis. The transcript is part of Labadie Collection, Single Vertical Files, Folder: Anarchism, Warren Josiah. Due to its archival character, there are no alterations and the punctuation has been left in its original version.

After a long time he managed to get into the type-casting department of the Cincinnati Type Foundry at the corner of Vine and Fifth Streets, (where it is still in operation). By close observation he caught the idea of the type-mould, and going to work, he succeeded in making a type-mould and all his patterns, with everything appertaining to the different fonts of type. Well I remember, in 1845,[354] when I was a little chap, I watched my father making type at the same fireplace at which my mother cooked the meals. For days, months and ye- rs did my father work to enable himself to publish his paper –"The Peaceful Revolutionist". Then in 1832[355] the cholera first made its appear-nee, and I well remember how my father set up his type and printed hand-bills cautioning the people how to live during the prevalence of that disease. These bills described the symptoms and how to treat them. Then I was allowed to go with my father to scatter the bills of caution along the streets, and I remember how proud

I was when those who saw what my father was doing, shook hands with him so warmly. What with his work of printing precautionary notices and attending a large number of funerals with masonic lodges, firemen and other organizations requiring bands, my father was kept busy for days and weeks and months, there was scarcely an hour that a funeral didn't take place. Time went on, so did deaths, but our family lived through It. Fortunately for the writer, being only six years o f a g e. could not realize the state of affairs, nor the horror of the situation. He trotting along scattering broadcast the "caution" notices proud of telling how many papers he had given to the people each day. If the city records of 1832-1834 were not destroyed during the destruction of the court house some years ago, the thanks of the city alderman to him will be found recorded to Josiah Warren if I mistake not. I should have stated that when my father left New Harmony and went to Cincinnati in 1837 he leased from Mr. Longworth (a gentleman well remembered by old inhabitants of Cincinnati as one of the largest real-estate owners of the city) a tract of land lying between Elm and John and from 5th to 9th, for 99 years. Had he not become a "reformer" of the labor question and a student of the problem of "Peaceful Revolution", he might, with his knowledge of business have lived and died a rich man, but as his convictions as to the right and liberties of the laboring classes generally became more confirmed he concluded this purchase of land to hold for a profit, all wrong, so he resumed the 99 year lease to Mr. Longvorth. Time went on. Finally some friends, who were interested in his "Labor for Labor" ideas, joined in his movements, and he was induced to move to Trenton, Ohio, with the idea of starting a community to be run on the "Labor for Labor" system, but after building a comfortable residence within a mile of Trenton, and living there for some three years, he found we were too remote from those who were interested in these things, so in 1838 we moved back to New Harmony, and he applied himself to simplifying the art of printing. About this time he found that in

---

[354] The date is crossed out, and there is a question mark in the margin.
[355] The date is underlined in the manuscript.

order to build such a press as he contemplated and Ills ambition dictated, It was necessary for him to go to Cincinnati that he could have his work done, and some time in March he went to Cincinnati, taking me with him. He soon had his work room for *the* iron work and machinery, also cabinet shops, office and printing office for job work such as business cards, advertisements, etc. *The* writer, then only 13 years of age did the typesetting end card-printing; this work was done on one of my father's job presses. The building where tills work was done, and where the, first [continuous] sheet press was ever built and worked, was in the middle of the magnificent block facing the splendid fountain on Fifth Street, the block at that time was considered a splendid structure, beings two stories high.

The work of building the press progressed rapidly for those times, and job printing was carried on by the writer. Finally the great and beautiful press was finished, and fully tested. It proved capable of striding off from forty to sixty copies per minute, an achievement in printing never before heard of or imagined. As it was the intention to use this mammoth press for the presidential campaign, of 1840 as soon as it had been thoroughly tested, this magnificent printing press was placed on board the steamboat Rover on New Year's Eve, 1840, I shall never forget that night. It was cold, and a terrible wind, snow and a hail storm was in full blast as we pulled out from the wharf. As the Rover was the last boat which was expected to leave for some time she was well crowded with passengers. It got colder and colder, and the ice was forming rapidly. Finally we cut our way to shore several miles from Madison, Indiana, or 57 above Louisville.

In the morning we were informed by the Captain that the prospects were very flattering for a starve out or a walkout of seven miles to Madison and all hands started on a dismal walk through the snow, the beautiful snow. We made the trip – got to Louisville, stayed three days, and it kept freezing harder. As no stages were running, my father made arrangements to go in a sleigh, got up at 4 a.m., took the sleigh, rode three hours, stopped for breakfast, and finding we were nearly frozen we concluded to walk the balance of the way home – one hundred and seventy five miles. This distance we made on foot in six and a half days to New Harmony. It took the Rover over two months to do it, as she was icebound all that time.

Finally the press was placed in the office at Evansville. This beautiful machine opened up splendidly, but no sooner had my father returned home than the platen press jammers commenced their anarchistic devilment. They had never seen a press that would print more than four to six copies per minute and they were going to be d--m[356] If any bloody press should take the bread out of their mouths by doing the work in no time. So these scoundrels kept my father in hot water, till one day he engaged some wagons and had the press hauled home and broke it up.

In the meantime, between the 1840 presidential campaign and the destruction of the continuous sheet press (it was used, I believe for about two years) my father

---

[356] Illegible.

started the "time store". It was located in the building that stood contiguous to where the magnificent New Harmony Institute just erected (which is the generous gift of Dr. Murphy). The time store was started by my father for the purpose of illustrating the labor for labor system. The goods he bought principally of Evansville merchants. The customers would come in and ask for what was wanted. The time dial was set to correspond with the minute hand of the clock and when the customer was through with his purchase, the time required in waiting on him was figured up, this labor was paid by the customer in labor notes, and the cost of the goods was paid in cash. There was no profit added to the first cost of the goods, except the amount expended in freight bills and other incidentals. The labor notes, of course, represented all classes, merchants, farmers, doctors and every descriptive of labor, and the rates per hour were regulated by the cost to the person of having to spend the time in learning the business in which he was engaged. I-remember that a large number of the citizens of the town and country contiguous used to meet once every two weeks t the "Hall" fitted up in a large building called "No. 1" which belonged to my father. In this were also the shops where the "library printing presses, type cases, etc. were being made.

The friends of the labor movement met, and the question was discussed, the price- of different kinds of labor suggested, and acted upon. This was continued for a time, but of course it beings-only an illustration of the "labor for labor" idea, in about two years this was dropped, and, as father had received from his friend Robert Dale Owen's large amount of property in buildings and land for an interest in the undertaking, and as my father concluded that his friend, Mr. Owen, had not gotten value received, he decided to deed back to Mr. Oven the whole of that property, how many men would have done this? He then bought property about a mile out on the hills and building a residence, devoted himself to a new method of sterotyping, spent time and money, and his work was the first of the kind which developed into the present system of electro-typing.

Being a fine musician, he saw that the art of music was much retarded by the intricacy of the present method of musical notation His method was all right. It dispensed with the sharp and flat s signatures and the tier and length of the stem gave the length of the note, and the piano or forte power was designated by the size of the note itself.

But the fallacy of the introduction of any new method of musical notation is prominently apparent when we are cognizant of the fact that the whole world has but one system of musical notation, also the whole world has used no other since the art developed into an art.

My father, however, spent a great deal of time in making plate by means of his own invention, to print his system of musical notation, previous to his going to Boston. He went there in 1857[357] and interested himself in developing a printing process, by which the type plate was on a cylinder, and this system of printing was

---

[357] Handwritten information 1858 in the margin.

used in Washington City, I believe, the surface of the plate being a composition of Gum Shellac with other ingredients. Devoting himself to the advancement of civilization, he died in Boston in 1875,[358] having gone through a [chequered] life, and for many years a fine musician. I never knew him to use profane language or to touch liquor of any kind, or use tobacco in any form. He was strictly temperance in every respect.

---

[358] 1874 written in the margin.

BIBLIOGRAPHY

Primary sources and archival materials written by Josiah Warren

- *To the Friends of Social System, Cycle of 8 Articles Written between June 1ˢᵗ and July 27ᵗʰ 1827.* signed "A Late Member of New Harmony".
- "Time-Magazine." *New Harmony Gazette* 26 Dec. 1827: 94.
- "To the Public." *Mechanics' Free Press* 10 May 1828: 2, col. B.
- "Untitled letter to the editor, dated April 20ᵗʰ, 1828." *Mechanics' Free Press* 10 May 1828: 2, col. B C.
- "Plan of the Cincinnati Labour for Labour Store." *Mechanics' Free Press* 9 Aug. 1828): 1, col. A.
- "From the March of Mind." New Harmony Gazette 10 Sept. 1828: 365.
- "Time Store." *Western Tiller* 12 September 1828: 20.
- "Time System for Labor Exchange." *Western Tiller*, cycle of 5 articles Sept/Oct 1828.
- *Reduction in the Cost of Printing Apparatus*, Cincinnati: Josiah Warren, 1830.
- "Communications. Printing in Family." *The Free Enquirer* 13 Mar. 1830: 157.
- "Communications. Improvement in the Machinery of Law." *The Free Enquirer* 17 July 1830: 300--301.
- "To the Friends of the Equal Exchange of Labor in the West." *Free Enquirer* 17 July 1830: 301--302.
- "Equal Exchange of Labor." *Free Enquirer* 17 July 1830: 308.
- "A Working Man, on equal exchange of labor." *New York Sentinel and Working Man's Advocate* 11 Aug. 1830: 1. Unsigned, ascribed to Warren.
- "Reply to E. C." *The Free Enquirer* 14 Aug. 1830: 332.
- "Social Experiment." *The Free Enquirer* 26 Feb. 1831: 137-138.
- "Written on Hearing of the Death of Camilla Wright." *The Free Enquirer* 23 Feb. 1833: 144.
- "Of our state difficulties." *Peaceful Revolutionist* 1, no. 2 (February 1833): 6.
- "Principles and progress of an experiment of rational social intercourse." *Peaceful Revolutionist* 1, no. 2 (February 1833): 7.
- "Society as it is." *Peaceful Revolutionist* 1, no. 2 (February 1833): 8.
- "Individuality." *Peaceful Revolutionist* 5 Apr. 1833: 13.
- "A brush at old Cobwebs." *Peaceful Revolutionist* 5 Apr. 1833: 14.
- "State of Things in 1833." *Reformer and Christian* 13 no. 3 (Apr 1833), p. 34.
- *Introduction to a New Printing Apparatus, Adapted to the Wants and Capacities of Private Citizens.* Trenton, Tuscarawas County, Ohio: Josiah Warren, 1836.
- *Manifesto*, New Harmony: J. Warren, 1841.
- *Herald of Equity* 1, no. 1 (1841).
- *Gazette of Equitable Commerce* 1, no. 2, (September 1842).
- *A New System of Notation: Intended to Promote the More General Cultivation & More Just Performance of Music.* New Harmony: Warren, 1843.
- *Letter on Equitable Commerce.* New Harmony: Warren's Amateur Print, 1844.
- *A Collection of the Most Popular Church Music Written Upon Geometric or Scientific Principles.* New Harmony, 1844.

- *Equitable Commerce: A New Development of Principles, as Substitutes for Laws and Governments. Proposed as Elements of New Society.* New Harmony, 1846.
- *Equitable Commerce: A New Development of Principles, for the Harmoneous Adjustment and Regulation of the Pecuniary, Intellectual, and Moral Intercourse of Mankind: Proposed as Elements of New Society.* Utopia, Ohio: Amos E. Senter 1849. 2nd Edition.
- "Letter from Josiah Warren." *Boston Investigator* 25 Sept. 1849: 3.
- "Equitable Commerce. No. II." *Boston Investigator* 10 Oct, 1849: lack of page numbers, col. C.
- "Equitable Commerce. No. III. What Constitutes the Just Reward of Labor?" *Boston Investigator* 31 Oct. 1849: lack of page numbers, col. C.
- "A few Words about: What Constitutes the Just Reward of Labor." *Boston Investigator* 14 Nov. 1849: 1. Signed "Worker".
- "Equitable Commerce. No. IV." *Boston Investigator* 21 Nov. 1849: 2.
- "Equitable Commerce." *Boston Investigator* 10 Sept. 1851: col. C.
- *Equitable Commerce: A New Development of Principles as Substitutes for Laws and Governments Proposed as Elements of New Society.* New York: Fowlers and Wells, 1852. With Stephen Pearl Andrews.
- *Practical Details in Equitable Commerce: Showing the Workings, in Actual Experiment, During a Series of Years, of the Social Principles Expounded in the Works Called "Equitable Commerce," by the Author of this, and "The Science Of Society," by Stephen P. Andrews.* Vol. 1. New York: Fowlers and Wells, 1852.
- "A Brief Outline of Equitable Commerce." *Boston Investigator* 28 Apr. 1852: 4.
- *Positions Defined.* Village of Modern Times 1854.
- "Explanation." *Boston Investigator* 22 Feb. 1854: 2.
- "To Enquirers." *Periodical Letter* (August 1854): 20.
- *Periodical Letter on the Principles and Progress of the Equity Movement,* Josiah Warren, Thompson P.O., Long Island, N.Y. (Vol. 1, no. 1-8, 1854-1855), 2nd series, Vol. 1, No. 1-9, 1856-1857, Boston, Cliftondale).
- *Written Music Remodeled, and Invested with the Simplicity of an Exact Science.* Boston: J.P. Jewett, 1860.
- *The Principle of Equivalents: A Subject of Immediate and Serious Interest to Both Sexes and all Classes of all Nations.* Long Island, N.Y. or London, 1861. With A. C. Cuddon.
- *Modern Education.* Long Island, NY, 1861.
- *Modern Government and Its True Mission, a Few Words for the American Crisis,* 1862 [ascribed to Warren].
- *True Civilization an Immediate Necessity, and the Last Ground of Hope for Mankind: Being the Results and Conclusions of Thirty-nine years" Laborious Study and Experiments in Civilization as it is, and in Different Enterprises for Reconstruction.* Boston: J. Warren, 1863.
- "A Letter to Louis Kossuth." *Boston Investigator* 17 Feb. 1864: 321.
- *Principle (the) of Equivalents: Labor for Labor: The Most Disagreeable Labor, Entitled to the Highest Compensation.* London: A.C. Cuddon, 1869 [ascribed to Warren].
- *The Quarterly Letter: Devoted Mainly to Showing the Practical Applications and Progress of "Equity."* Cliftondale, Mass.: Josiah Warren, 1867.
- *The Former Title of this Work was "Equitable Commerce", but it is Now Ranked as the First Part of True Civilization: a Subject of Vital and Serious Interest to All People; but Most Immediately to the Men and Women of Labor and Sorrow ... Part 1.* Clintondale, Mass.: The Author, 1869.
- "Woman and the Money Question." *The Revolution,* 15 July 1869: 29.
- "Superficialities." *The Revolution* 12 Aug. 1869: 83.
- *Response to the Call of the National Labor Union for Essays on the Following Subjects...* Boston, 1871.
- *Political Platform for the Coming Party.* Boston: publisher not identified. Possibly Warren himself, 1871.
- "The Motives for Communism—How It Worked and What It Led To." – cycle of articles published in Woodhull and Claflin's Weekly 17 Feb. 1872 – 26 Apr. 1873.
- "To H.R., Texas." *Word* (July 1872): 1.

- *Practical Applications of the Elementary Principles of True Civilization to the Minute Details of Every Day Life: and the Facts and Conclusions of Forty Seven Years Study and Experiments in Reform Movements through Communism to and in Elementary Principles.* Princeton, Mass.: J. Warren, 1873.
- *Letter to E. H. Heywood.* Princeton, MA, 1873.
- "Labor for Labor." *Word* (Jan. 1873): 1.
- *Money: The Defects of Money Are the "Roots of All Evil."* Charlestown, MA, 1873.
- "The Cost Principle." *Index* 11 Dec. 1873: 504-505.
- "Josiah Warren's Last Letter." *Index* 30 Apr. 1874: 207-208.
- "Labor the Only Ground of Price." *Index* 28 May 1874: 260-261.
- *True Civilization; A Subject of Vital and Serious Interest to all People; but Most Immediately to the Men and Women of Labor and Sorrow.* Princeton: B.R. Tucker, 1875. With Stephen Pearl Andrews.

▪ Archival materials and manuscripts of other authors

- Agnes Inglis Papers, Labadie Collection, Special Collections Library, University of Michigan.
- Jo Labadie Papers, Labadie Collection, Special Collections Library, University of Michigan.
- A.J. MacDonald, *Collection of Utopian Materials*, General Collection, Beinecke Rare Book and Manuscript Library, Yale University.
- Stephen Pearl Andrews Papers, State Historical Society of Wisconsin, Madison, Wisconsin.
- Ed Weber Papers, uncatalogued materials, Labadie Collection, University of Michigan.
- Stact Papers, Clements Library, University of Michigan.
- New Harmony Correspondence 1812-1871, I and III series, Working Men's Institute of New Harmony, Indiana.

▪ Primary sources not written by Warren

- *1850 U.S. Federal Population Census*, Film number: 442944.
- "A letter from J P Davis," *Social Revolutionist, The. A Medium for the Free Discussion of General Principles and Practical Measures, Pertaining to Human Progress and General Well-Being* 3.4 (Apr. 1857): 108-110.
- "A List of Patents Issued from the 14th March to 11th April, 1846." *Scientific American* 1, no. 49 (August 271846): 1.
- "A New System of Notation." *American Journal of Music and Musical Visitor* 16 Feb. 1846: 47.
- "A peep into Modern Times." *The Circular, Published Weekly by the Oneida and Wallingford Community* 28 Dec. 1868: 324.
- Adams, John. *Diary and Autobiography of John Adams.* Vol. 3. Ed. L. H. Butterfield. Cambridge: Harvard University Press, 1961.
- "Address; Delivered by Robert Owen of New Lanark." *New Harmony Gazette* 1 Oct. 1825: 1.
- "Advertisement." *Boston Investigator* 7 Mar. 1849: 3.
- "Advertisement." *Nichols' Journal of Health, Water-cure and Human Progress* (Apr. 1853): 3, 7.
- "Advertisement." *Nichols' Journal of Health, Water-cure and Human Progress* (Aug. 1853): 37.
- Andrews, Stephen Pearl. "Phonotypy and Phonography, or Speech-Printing and Speech-Writing." *Boston Investigator* 3 Oct. 1849: 4.
- ———. "Equitable commerce. Cost, the scientific limit of price." *The Merchants' Magazine and Commercial Review* (Mar. 1851): 332.
- ———. *The Science of Society: The True Constitution of Government in the Sovereignty of the Individual As the Final Development of Protestantism, Democracy, and Socialism.* New York: William J. Baner, 1851.
- ———. "Warren's Social Theory--Reply to The Tribune." *New – York Daily Tribune* 23 July 1852: 6.
- ———. *The Science of Society no. 1, The True Constitution of Government in the Sovereignty of the Individual as the Final development of Protestantism, Democracy and Socialism.* New York: T. L. Nichols, 1854.

- ———. "The Sovereignty of Individual." *Periodical Letter* (Sept. 1857): 87.
- Andrews, Stephen Pearl, and James, Henry, and Greeley, Horace. *Love, Marriage, and Divorce, and the Sovereignty of the Individual. a Discussion by Henry James, Horace Greeley, and S. P. Andrews: Including the Final Replies of Mr. Andrews, Rejected by the Tribune. Edited by S. P. Andrews.* New York: Stringer & Townsend, 1853.
- ———. *Love, Marriage, and Divorce, and the Sovereignty of the Individual: A Discussion between Henry James, Horace Greeley, and Stephen Pearl Andrews.* Boston: B.R. Tucker, 1889.
- "Articles of Union And Cooperation." *New Harmony Gazette* 15 Feb. 1826: 162.
- "As Usual!." *Boston Investigator* 8 Feb. 1854: 2.
- Ballou, A., and Heywood, W. S. *History of the Hopedale Community: From Its Inception to Its Virtual Submergence in the Hopedale Parish.* Lowell, Mass.: Thompson & Hill, 1897.
- Ballou, A. *Practical Christian Socialism: a Conversational Exposition of the True System of Human Society, Etc.* Hopedale: Fowllers & Wells, 1854.
- Beck, William. *Money and Banking, or Their Nature and Effects Considered. Together with a Plan for the Universal Diffusion of Their Legitimate Benefits Without Their Evils. by a Citizen of Ohio.* Cincinnati: William Beck, 1839.
- Bentham, Jeremy. *Plan of Parliamentary Reform in the Form of a Catechism.* London: Printed for R. Hunter, 1817.
- ———. *The Works of Jeremy Bentham.* Vol. 6. Published under the Superintendence of his Executor, John Bowring. Edinburgh: William Tait, 1843.
- ———. *An Introduction to the Principles of Morals and Legislation,* Oxford: Clarendon Press, 1907.
- ———. *First Principles Preparatory to a Constitutional Code.* Ed. P. Schofield. Oxford: Clarendon Press, 1989.
- Blacker, Peter I. "Equitable Villages." *Boston Investigator* 21 Jan. 1852: 4.
- ———. "American Socialism." *Boston Investigator* 20 Oct. 1852: 1.
- ———. "An Outline of Equitable Commerce." *Boston Investigator* 5 Jan. 1853: 1.
- ———. "The Golden Rule." *Boston Investigator* 26 Oct. 1853: 3.
- ———. "Individualism Versus Institutionalism." *Boston Investigator* 16 Aug. 1854: 2.
- ———. "The Government Mania." *Boston Investigator* 2 May 1855: 2.
- ———. "Submission to the Will of the Majority." *Boston Investigator* 27 June 1855: 2.
- ———. "Secret Societies." *Boston Investigator* July 4, 1855: 1.
- ———. "The Perpetuity of the Union." *Boston Investigator* 25 July 1856: 2.
- Blanc, Louis. *The Organization of Work.* Trans. Marie Paula Dickoré, University of Cincinnati Studies 2, vol. 7 (1911), *Boston Investigator* 14 Mar. 1849: 3.
- *Boston Investigator* 21 Mar. 1849: 3.
- *Boston Investigator* 16 May 1849: col A.
- Bray J.F. *Labour's Wrongs and Labour's Remedy; or, the Age of Might and the Age of Right.* Leeds: David Green, Briggade, 1839.
- Brissot, W. J.-P. *Recherches philosophiques sur le droit de propriété: Considéré dans la nature ; pour servir de premier chapître à la Théorie des loix de M. Linguet.* Chartres, 1780.
- Brown, J. "Strikes after strike..." *The Crisis* 3 May 1834: 19.
- Brown, P. *Twelve Months in New-Harmony: Presenting a Faithful Account of the Principal Occurrences Which Have Taken Place There Within That Period; Interspersed with Remarks.* Cincinnati: W.H. Woodward, 1827.
- Brutus, "Messrs Editors—Among the Other Arrangements of Mr. Warren of Cincinnati, Published in Your Paper of Last Week, I Perceive That He Has Introduced into His Method of Conducting the Business of His Magazine, Labour Notes as a Circulating Medium." *Mechanics' Free Press* 23 Aug. 1828: col. C.
- Bryan, W. "Brighton Co-Operative Benevolent Fund Association." *Cooperative Magazine* (May 1827): 225.
- ———. "Brighton Co-Operative Benevolent Fund Association." *Cooperative Magazine* (Sept. 1827) 418-420.

▪ ———. "Brighton Co-Operative Benevolent Fund Association." *Cooperative Magazine* (Nov. 1827): 507-551.

▪ Buckminster, L. N. H. *The Hastings Memorial: a Genealogical Account of the Descendants of Thomas Hastings of Watertown, Mass. From 1634 to 1864. With an Appendix And Index.* Boston: Samuel G. Drake, 1866.

▪ Burke E., *List of Patents for Inventions And Designs, Issued by the United States, From 1790 to 1847: With the Patent Laws And Notes of Decisions of the Courts of the United States for the Same Period.* Washington: J&GS Gideon, 1847.

▪ Burke, Edmund. *The Inherent Evils of All State Governments Demonstrated; Being a Reprint of Edmund Burke's Celebrated Essay, Entitled: "a Vindication of Natural Society:" with Notes and an Appendix. [...].* London: Holyoake, 1858.

▪ ———. *Reflections on the Revolutions in France.* Chicago: Gateway ed., 1955.

▪ "Celebration of Fourier's Birthday in Boston." *Harbinger* 17 Apr. 1876: 208.

▪ Codman, Ch. *A Brief History of the City of Modern Times, Long Island, N.Y. and a Glorification of Some of its Saints.* Brentwood, NY, circa 1905. (manuscript in Modern Times Collection, Suffolk County Historical Society, Riverhead NY, the transcript encompass of 27 pages is in Huntington Library, Long Island NY).

▪ Common Sense, "The Sovereignty of the Individual." *Boston Investigator* 22 Aug. 1855: 2.

▪ "Constitution of the New Harmony Agricultural and Pastoral Society, Article I, Article II, Article III." *New Harmony Gazette* 9 Aug. 1826: 362.

▪ "Constitution of the New Harmony Community of Equality." *New Harmony Gazette* 15 Feb. 1826: 161.

▪ Conway, Moncure Daniel. *Autobiography Memories and Experiences of Moncure Daniel Conway: In Two Volumes.* Boston: Houghton, Mifflin and Company, 1904.

▪ "Co-operation." *The London Co-operative Magazine* (Nov. 1827): 509.

▪ Cridge, Alfred. "Present position and future prospect of American socialism", *The Social Revolutionist; A Medium for the Free Discussion of General Principles and Practical Measures, Pertaining to Human Progress and General Well-Being* 1 (January 1856): 10.

▪ "Dual Commerce Association." *The Circular* 17 Feb. 1859: 4.

▪ Duckett, W. *Dictionnaire de la conversation et de la lecture: Inventaire raisonne des notions generales les plus indispensables a tous, par une societe de savants et de gens de lettres, sous la dir. de M.W.Duckett. 2e ed.corr.et augm. de plusieurs milliers d'articles d'actualite.* Paris: Didot, 1863.

▪ Dunn, J. P., and Kemper, G. W. H. *Indiana and Indianans: A History of Aboriginal and Territorial Indiana and the Century of Statehood.* Chicago: American Historical Society, 1919.

▪ Dwight, J.S., *Music in Boston* [w:] *The Memorial History of Boston: Including Suffolk County, Massachusetts, 1630-1880.* Vol. 4. Ed. J. Winsor. Boston: Osgood & Co., 1881.

▪ E. C. "Communications." *The Free Enquirer* 14 Aug. 1830: 332.

▪ Edger, Henry. *Modern Times, the Labor Question, and the Family: A Brief Statement of Facts and Principles by Henry Edger.* New York: Calvin Blanchard, 1855.

▪ Emerson, Ralph Waldo, and Carlyle, Thomas. *The Correspondence of Thomas Carlyle and Ralph Waldo Emerson.* Vol. 1. Boston: J. R. Osgood and Co., 1883.

▪ Engels, Friedrich. Socialism: Utopian and Scientific, in K. Marx and F. Engels, Collected Works, vol. 24, (London, 1988).

▪ "Equitable Commerce." *Liberator* 14 Sept. 1855: 146.

▪ Fourier, Charles. *The Theory of the Four Movements.* Eds. Gareth Stedman Jones and Ian Patterson. Cambridge: Cambridge University Press, 1996.

▪ "Free Love." *The United States Magazine of Science, Art, Manufactures, Agriculture, Commerce and Trade* (Nov. 1855): 204.

▪ G. "Communism the Only Alternative." *The Circular* 4 Aug. 1852: 154.

▪ *Genealogy: a Weekly Journal of American Ancestry* 1, no 6 (1912).

▪ Godwin, W. *An Inquiry Concerning Political Justice: And Its Influence on General Virtue and Happiness.* London: Printed for G. G. J. and J. Robinson, 1793.

▪ Gray, John. *A Lecture on Human Happiness Being the First of a Series of Lectures on that Subject, in which Will be Comprehended a General Review of the Causes of the Existing Evils of Society, and a Development of Means by which They May be Permanently and Effectually Removed. To which are Added The Articles of Agreement Drawn Up and Recommended by the London Co-operative Society for the Formation of a Community on Principles of Mutual Co-operation, Within Fifty Miles of London*. London: Sherwood, Johnes & Co., 1825.

■ ———. *The social system: A treatise on the principle of exchange*. Edinburgh: W. Tait, 1831.

■ Gouge, W. M., and Dorfman, J. *A Short History of Paper Money and Banking in the United States, to which is Prefixed an Inquiry into the Principles of the System*. New York: Kelley, 1968.

■ Herbert, William. *A Visit to the Colony of Harmony in Indiana... Recently Purchased by Mr. Owen for the Establishment of a Society of Mutual Co-operation and Community of Property: in a Letter to a Friend: to which are Added Some Observations on that Mode of Society and on Political Society at Large: also a Sketch for the Formation of a Co-operative Society*. London: Printed for G. Mann, 1825.

■ Heywood, Ezra H. *The Great Strike: Its Relations to Labor, Property, and Government. Suggested by the Memorable Events which, Originating in the Tyrannous Extortion of Railway Masters, and the Execution of Eleven Labor Reformers, called "Mollie Maguires," June 21, 1877, Culminated in Burning the Corporation Property, in Pittsburg, July 22, Following*. Princeton, Mass.: Co-operative Publishing Co., 1878.

■ *History of Greene County, New York: With Biographical Sketches of Its Prominent Men*. New York: J.B. Beers & Co., 1884.

■ Hobbes, Thomas. *The English Works of Thomas Hobbes of Malmesbury*. Vol. 3. London: J. Bohn, 1839.

■ ———. *Leviathan: Or, the Matter, Forme and Power of a Commonwealth, Ecclesiasticall and Civil*. Ed. M. Oakeshott. Oxford: Blackwell, 1946.

■ *Indiana Statesman*, 1 Feb. 1845.

■ Ingalls, Joshua K. *Henry George Examined: Should Land Be Nationalized or Individualized?*. New York: Published by the author, 1882.

■ ———. *Social Wealth: The Sole Factors and Exact Ratios in Its Acquirement and Apportionment*. New York: Social Science Pub. Co., 1885.

■ ———. *Economic Equities: a Comend of the Natural Laws of Industrial Production and Exchange*. New York: Social Science Pub. Co., 1887.

■ ———. *Reminiscences of an Octogenarian in the Fields of Industrial and Social Reform*, M.L. Holbrook, New York 1897.

■ J H N [John Humphrey Noyes], "Letter from a Free-lover." *Circular* 27 Jun. 1870: 116.

■ J.H.N. [John Humphrey Noyes] "Individual Sovereignty." *Circular* 6 Jun. 1870: 1.

■ J. P. "Moral Philosophy." *Peaceful revolutionists* 5 Apr. 1833: 16.

■ James, C.L., *Origin of Anarchism*. Chicago: A. Isaak Publisher, 1902.

■ Jefferson, Thomas. "Notes on the State of Virginia, Query XIX, The present state of manufactures, commerce, interior and exterior trade?" *The Writings of Thomas Jefferson*. Vol. 4. Ed. P. L. Ford. New York: G.P. Putnam's Sons, 1904.

■ Jevons, W. S. *Money and the Mechanism of Exchange*. New York: D. Appleton, 1875.

■ Johnson, Alexander B., *The Philosophy of Human Knowledge; or, A Treatise on Language: A Course of Lectures Delivered at the Utica Lyceum*. New York: G. & C. Carvill, 1828.

■ ———. *A Treatise on Language: Or, the Relation Which Words Bear to Things, in Four Parts*. New York: Harper & Brothers, 1836.

■ "Josiah Warren—and 'R. H.'" *Boston Investigator* 25 July 1849: 2.

■ "Josiah Warren" *Woodhull and Claflin's Weekly* 14 June 1874: 12.

■ Jourdain, R. J., *Man's Mission on Earth: Series of Lectures Delivered at Dr. Jourdan's Parisian Gallery of Anatomy Addressed to Those Laboring Under the Baneful Effects of Self-Abuse, Excesses Or Infection; Also, A Familiar Explanation of The Venereal Disease Showing The Danger Arising From Neglect or Improper Treatment in Disorders of the Generative System*. Buffalo: Warren, Johnson & Co., Printers, 1872.

■ Kellogg, Miner K., *Miner K. Kellogg: Recollections of New Harmony*. Ed. L. L. Sylvester. "Indiana Magazine of History 64 (1968): 39-64.

- Kelpius, Johannes, and Richards, Kirby. *A Method of Prayer: A Mystical Pamphlet from Colonial America*. Philadelphia: Schuylkill Wordsmiths, 2006.
- "Labor for Labor." *The Revolution* 5 Aug. 1869: 71.
- "Lecture by Josiah Warren (News)." *Boston Investigator* 17 Jan. 1849: col. B.
- Leland, T.C. "Individual Sovereignty." *American Socialism* 1 June 1876: 73.
- "Literary." *The Independent … Devoted to the Consideration of Politics, Social and Economic Tendencies, History, Literature, and the Arts* 16 Jan. 1851: 16.
- Locke, John. Two Treatises of Government. Ed. P. Laslett. New York: Cambridge University Press, 1960.
- M. P. S., "A Letter from Utopia." *Boston Investigator* 1 May 1850: 3.
- Maistre, Joseph de. *Oeuvres complètes*. Vol. 14. Lyon: Vitte et Perrussel 1886.
- Masquerier, Lewis. *Sociology, Or, the Reconstruction of Society, Government, and Property: Upon the Principles of the Equality, the Perpetuity, and the Individuality of the Private Ownership of Life, Person, Government, Homestead, and the Whole Product of Labor, by Organizing All Nations into Townships of Self-Governed Homestead Democracies-Self-Employed in Farming and Mechanism, Giving All the Liberty and Happiness to Be Found on Earth*. New York: The author, 1877.
- Mill, John Stuart. (1848). *Principles of Political Economy with some of their Applications to Social Philosophy*, ed. William James Ashley (London: Longmans, Green and Co., 1909).
- ———. *Collected Works of John Stuart Mill*. Volume I – *Autobiography*. Ed. John M. Robson. Toronto: University of Toronto Press, 1981.
- ———. *The Collected Works of John Stuart Mill, Volume X – Essays on Ethics, Religion, and Society*. Ed. John M. Robson. Toronto: University of Toronto Press; London: Routledge and Kegan Paul, 1985.
- "Modern Times — A New City." *Boston Investigator* 30 June 1852: 4.
- "Mr. Warren's Lecture." *Boston Investigator* 24 Jan. 1849: 3.
- *New Harmony Gazette* 5 Dec. 1827: 70.
- "New Harmony Sunday Meeting for Instruction in the New System, August 26, 1826." *New Harmony Gazette* 16 Aug. 1826: 372.
- *New-York Daily Tribune* 30 Jan. 1855.
- *New-York Daily Tribune* 16 Oct. 1855: 5.
- *New-York Daily Tribune* 24 Oct. 1855: 4.
- *New-York Daily Tribune* 1 Dec. 1852: 5.
- *New-York Daily Tribune* 16 Dec. 1852: 5.
- *New-York Daily Tribune* 18 Dec. 1852: 5.
- *New-York Daily Tribune* 8 Nov. 1858: 3.
- *New-York Daily Tribune* 18 Sept. 1852: 6.
- Nichols Mary G., "Dress, Marriage: Defining Positions." *Nichols' Journal of Health, Water-cure and Human Progress* (May 1853): 13.
- Nichols, Mary G. or Nichols, Thomas Low?. "Living up to principle." *Nichols' Journal of Health, Water-cure and Human Progress* (Dec. 1854): 158.
- ———. "Marriage: Defining Positions." *Nichols' Journal of Health, Water-cure and Human Progress* (Jan. 1855): 31.
- Nichols, Thomas Low. *Woman in All Ages and Nations: A Complete and Authentic History of the Manners and Customs, Character and Condition of the Female Sex, in Civilized and Savage Countries, from the Earliest Ages to the Present Time*. New York: Long & Brother, 1849.
- ———. *Woman in All Ages and Nations: A Complete and Authentic History of the Manners and Customs, Character and Condition of the Female Sex*. New York: Fowlers and Wells 1852.
- ———. "City of Modern Times." *Nichols' Journal of Health, Water-cure and Human Progress* (Aug. 1853): 39.
- ———. *Forty Years of American Life. In Two Volumes – Volume I-II*. London: J. Maxwell and Co., 1864.
- Nichols, Thomas Low?. "To the World's reformers." *Nichols' Journal of Health, Water-cure and Human Progress* (July 1853): 31.

- Nichols, Thomas Low, and Nichols, Mary G. "Calumny." *Nichols' Journal of Health, Water-cure and Human Progress* (Sept. 1853): p. 44-46.
- ———. *Marriage: Its History, Character, and Results. Its Sanctity and Its Profanities, Its Science and Its Facts, Demonstrating Its Influence as a Civilized Institution on the Happiness of the Individual and the Progress of the Race.* Cincinatti: V. Nicholson, 1854.
- "Notice." *Boston Investigator* 24 Jan. – 21 Feb. 1849: 3.
- "Notice." *Boston Investigator* 16 May 1849: 2.
- "Notice." *Boston Investigator* 25 Sept. 1849: 3.
- "On The Mis-Statement of the St. Simonians On The Subject Of "Community" To The Editor Of The Pioneer." *Pioneer* 1 Mar. 1834.Orvis, J. "Equitable Commerce Association." *Liberator* 21 Sept. 1855: 150.
- ———. "Equitable Commerce." *Liberator* 28 Sept. 1855: 154.
- "Our Muck-Heap, No. V." *Circular* 9 Nov. 1868: 268.
- "Our Muck-Heap, No. VI." *Circular* 16 Nov. 1868: 276.
- "Our Muck-Heap, No. XII. Josiah Warren. The New Harmony Time Store. A Peep Into Utopia. Individualism In A Brick-Yard. A Peep Into Modern Times." *Circular* 28 Dec. 1868: 324.
- Owen, Robert. *Report to the County of Lanark, of a Plan for Relieving Public Distress: And Removing Discontent, by Giving Permanent, Productive Employment, to the Poor and Working Classes, under Arrangements which will Essentially Improve their Character, and Ameliorate their Condition, Diminish the Expenses of Production and Consumption, and Create Markets Co-extensive with Production* (Glasgow: Printed at the University Press, for Wardlaw & Cunninghame, 1821).
- ———. *A Discourse on a New System of Society: As Delivered in the Hall of Representatives of the United States, in Presence of the President of the United States, the President Elect, Heads of Departments, Members of Congress, &c. &c., on the 25th of February, 1825.* Washington: Gales & Seaton, 1825.
- ———. "The Social System." *New Harmony Gazette* 21 Feb. 1827: 161.
- ———. *Threading My Way: Twenty-seven Years of Autobiography.* New York: G.W. Carleton & Co., 1874.
- ———. *A New View of Society and other Writings.* Ed Gregory Claeys. Harmondsworth: Penguin, 1991.
- "Paine Celebration at Modern Times, N. Y." *Boston Investigator* 8 Mar. 1854: 1.
- Pare, W. "Equitable Villages in America." Journal of the Statistical Society of London 19, no 2 (1856): 127-143.
- Pears, Thomas C., and Pears, Sarah. *New Harmony, an Adventure in Happiness: Papers of Thomas and Sarah Pears.* Indianapolis: Indiana historical Society, 1933.
- "People's Sunday Meeting." *Boston Investigator* 17 Jan. 1849: 3.
- "People's Sunday Meeting." *Boston Investigator* 28 Feb. 1849: 3.
- "People's Sunday Meeting." *Boston Investigator* 7 Mar. 1849: 3.
- "People's Sunday Meeting." *Boston Investigator* 14 Mar. 1849: 3.
- "People's Sunday Meeting." *Boston Investigator* 21 Mar. 1849: 3.
- Pickering, J. *The Working Man's Political Economy: Founded upon the Principle of Immutable Justice and the Inalienable Rights of Man; Designed for the Promotor of National Reform.* Cincinnati: Stereotyped in Warren's new patent method by Thomas Varney, 1847.
- Plekhanov, Georgiï V. *Anarchism and Socialism.* Chicago: C.H. Kerr & Co., 1909.
- "Political, Equitable Commerce." *The Literary Union; a Journal of Progress, in Literature and Education, Religion and Politics, Science and Agriculture* 7 Jul. 1849: 218-219.
- Proudhon, Pierre-Joseph. *Qu'est-ce que c'est que la propriété, ou, Recherches sur le principe du droit et du gouvernement.* Paris: Prévot, 1841.
- ———. *Système des contradictions économiques ou Philosophie de la misère,* 1846.
- ———. *Avertissement Aux Propriétaires, Ou: Lettre À M. Considérant, Rédacteur De La Phalange Sur Une Défense De La Propriété.* Paris: Garnier, 1848.
- ———. *Résumé De La Question Sociale, Banque D'échange.* Paris: Garnier, 1849.
- ———. *Lettres sur la philosophie du progress.* Bruxelles: Alphonse Lebegue, 1853.

■ ———. *System of Economical Contradictions; Or, the Philosophy of Misery.* Transl. Benjamin R. Tucker. Boston: B.R. Tucker, 1888.

■ ———. *General Idea of Revolution in the Nineteenth Century.* Trans. John B. Robinson. New York: Haskell House Publishers, 1969.

■ ———. *What is Property?.* Eds. D. R. Kelley and B. G. Smith. Cambridge: Cambridge University Press, 1994.

■ Proudhon, Pierre-Joseph, Charles A. Dana, William B. Greene, and Henry Cohen. *Proudhon's Solution of the Social Problem.* New York: Vanguard Press, 1927.

■ Proudhon, Pierre-Joseph, and McKay, Iain. *Property Is Theft!: A Pierre-Joseph Proudhon Anthology.* Baltimore: AK Press, 2011.

■ Proudhon, Pierre-Joseph, and Tucker, Benjamin R. *The Works of P.J. Proudhon, Vol. 1, What is Property?: An Inquiry into the Principle of Right and of Government.* Princeton, Mass.: Benj. R. Tucker, 1876.

■ "Review." *The Northern Star and National Trades' Journal* 28 Nov. 1846.

■ Ricardo, David. *On the Principles of Political Economy and Taxation.* Ed. P. Srafta, Cambridge: Cambridge University Press, 1981.

■ Ripley, G. "New publications." *New   York Daily Tribune* 3 Jul. 1852: 10.

■ Rockey, J. L. *History of Clermont County, Ohio, with Illustrations and Biographical Sketches of Its Prominent Men and Pioneers.* Philadelphia: L.H. Everts, 1880.

■ Rodbertus, J.K., "Die Forderungen der arbeitenden Klassen (1837)." *J. K Rodbertus. Zur Beleuchtung der Sozialen Frage.* Vol. 2. Berlin: Puttkammer & Muehlbrecht 1885. 195-223.

■ ———. *Zur Erkenntnis unserer staatswirthschaftlichen Zustände.* Neubrandenburg: G. Barnewitz, 1842.

■ Rouen, P. J. "Examen de un nouvelle ouvrage de M. Dunoyer Ancien Rédacteur du Censeur Européen parts 1. " *Le Producteur, journal de l'industrie, des sciences et des beaux-arts* 2 (1826): 158-170.

■ *Rules And Regulations for the Government of the Library Belonging to the New Harmony Working Men" Institute: With a Catalogue of Its Books.* New Harmony, Indiana, 1847.

■ Saint-Simon, Henri de. *The Political Thought of Saint-Simon.* Ed. Ghiţa Ionescu. Oxford: Oxford University Press, 1976.

■ Skidmore, T. *The Rights of Man to Property!: Being a Proposition to Make it Equal among the Adults of the Present Generation, and to Provide for its Equal Transmission to Every Individual of Each Succeeding Generation on Arriving at the Age of Maturity: Addressed to the Citizens of the State of New-York, Particularly, and to the People of Other States and Nations, Generally.* New-York: Printed for the author by A. Ming, Jr., 1829.

■ Smith, Adam. *The Glasgow Edition of the Works and Correspondence of Adam Smith vol. 1-2 An Inquiry into the Nature and Causes of the Wealth of Nations: Vol. 1-2.* W. B. Todd (Ed.) Oxford: Clarendon, 1975.

■ Smith, J. E. *Crisis* 28 Dec. 1833.

■ "Something New." *The Penny Satirist*, 25 Apr. 1840: 3.

■ Spooner, L., *Constitutional Law Relative to Credit, Currency and Banking.* Worcester, Mass.: J. B. Ripley Pub., 1843.

■ ———. *Poverty: Its Illegal Causes and Legal Cure.* Boston, Bella March, 1846.

■ ———. *The Law of Intellectual Property, or, An Essay On the Right of Authors and Inventors to Perpetual Property in Their Discoveries and Inventions* Boston: Bela Marsh, 1855.

■ ———. *Vices Are Not Crimes: A Vindication of Moral Liberty.* Cupertino: TANSTAAFL, 1977.

■ Sprading, Charles T. *Liberty and the Great Libertarians. An Anthology on Liberty, a Handbook of Freedom.* Los Angeles: published for the author, 1913.

■ Stein, L. von. *Der Sozialismus und Kommunismus des heutigen Frankreichs.* Leipzig: O. Wigand, 1848.

■ Stoehr, T. *Free Love in America: A Documentary History*, New York: AMS Press, 1979.

■ Taney, R. B., and Henry, J. *Fifth Annual Report of the Board of Regents of the Smithsonian Institution: To the Senate and House of Representatives, Showing the Operations, Expenditures, and Condition of the Institution, During the Year 1850. March 1, 1851. Read. March 7, 1851. Ordered, That the*

Report of the Smithsonian Institution Be Printed; and That Three Thousand Additional Copies Be Printed-One Thousand Copies of Which for the Use of the Smithsonian Institution. Washington (lack of publisher), 1851.

- "The Constitution of the Preliminary Society of New Harmony (The Society is instituted generally to promote the Happiness of the World)." *New Harmony Gazette* 1 Oct. 1825: 2-3
- *The Dual Commerce Association: its Experience, Results, Plans & Prospectus: First Report.* Boston: Dual Commerce Association, 1859.
- "The Unitary Home." *The Circular* 14 Apr. 1859: 4.
- Thompson, W. *An Inquiry into the Principles of the Distribution of Wealth Most Conducive to Human Happiness.* London: Longman, Hurst, Rees, Orme, Brown and Green; and Wheatley and Adlard, 1824.
- "To the World's reformers." *Nichols' Journal of Health, Water-cure and Human Progress* (July 1853): 31.
- Tocqueville Alexis de. *Democracy in America.* Trans. Henry Reeve. Philadelphia: J. & H. G. Langley, New York: Thomas, Cowperthwaite & Co. etc., 1840.
- Truth, "Cause and Effect," *The Revolution* 29 July 1869: 52.
- Tucker, Benjamin R. "On picked duty." *Liberty, not the Daughter but the Mother of Order* 6 Mar. 1886: 1.
- ———. "State Socialism and Anarchy." *Liberty, not the Daughter but the Mother of Order* 10 Mar. 1888: 3.
- ———. "Protection and its Relation to Rent." *Liberty, not the Daughter but the Mother of Order* 27 Oct. 1888: 4.
- ———. "On Picked Duty." *Liberty, not the Daughter but the Mother of Order* 14 (Dec. 1900): 1.
- Underhill, E. F. "Cost the limit of price." *Liberator* 14 Oct. 1853: 164.
- Untitled. *United States Magazine and Democratic Review* 6 (1839): 208-209.
- Untitled. *Spiritual telegraph* 23 Apr. 1853 (unpaginated).
- Untitled. *Nichols' Journal of Health, Water-cure and Human Progress* (Aug. 1853): 37.
- Untitled. *The Vaneguards* 1, no. 15 (June 1857): 115.
- Villager. "PORT CHESTER: Dr. Nichols's Water Cure Establishment – A General Stampede among the Female Pupils..." *New York Daily Tribune* 21 Jul. 1853: 5.
- *Vital Records of Lynn, MA, to the End of the Year 1849: Marriages and Death.* Vol. 2. Salem: The Essex Institute, 1909.
- Warren, G. W. *Josiah Warren,* November 10, 1893, Evansville, unpublished manuscript. New Harmony, Indiana (the original manuscript is deposited in Workingmen's Institute Library, the transcript is in Labadie Collectiion at the University of Michigan).
- "Weekly Summary." *The Plough Boy, and Journal of the Board of Agriculture* 26 May 1821: 415.
- Winthrop, J., and Hosmer, J. K. *Winthrop's Journal, "History of New England," 1630-1649.* New York: C. Scribner's Sons, 1908.
- *Woodhull & Claflin's Weekly* 13 May 1871: 8.
- *Woodhull & Claflin's Weekly* 3 June 1871: 6.
- *Word* (Aug. 1872). 1.
- Wright, F., *The Free Enquirer* 22 May 1830.

Secondary sources:

- Alican, Necip Fikri. *Mill's Principle of Utility: A Defense of John Stuart Mill's Notorious Proof* Amsterdam: Rodopi, 1994.
- Amoudruz, Madeleine. *Proudhon et l'Europe. Les Ideés de Proudhon en Politique Étrangère.* Paris: Éditions Domat Montchrestien, 1945.
- Ansart, Pierre. "Proudhon À Travers Le Temps." *L'homme et Société* 123-124 (1997): 17-24.
- Appleby, Joyce. "Liberalism and the American Revolution." *New England Quarterly,* (Mar. 1976): 3-26.
- ———. "The Social Origins of American Revolutionary Ideology." *Journal of American History,* 64 (1978): 935-958.

- ———. *Capitalism and a New Social Order: The Republican Vision of the 1790s.* New York: New York University Press, 1984.
- ———. "The Vexed Story of Capitalism Told by American Historians." *Journal of the Early Republic* 21 (2001): 1-18.
- Arieli, Yehoshua. *Individualism and Nationalism in American Ideology.* Cambridge: Harvard University Press, 1964.
- Aron, Stephen. "Pioneers and Profiteers: Land Speculation and the Homestead Ethic in Frontier Kentucky." *The Western Historical Quarterly* 23, no. 2 (1992): 179-198.
- Atack, Jeremy, and Bateman, Fred. *To Their Own Soil: Agriculture in the Antebellum North.* Ames: Iowa State University Press, 1987.
- ———. "Yeoman Farming: Antebellum America's Other 'Peculiar Institution'." *Agriculture and National Development: Views on the Nineteenth Century.* Ed. Lou Ferleger. Ames: Iowa State University Press, 1990. 25-51.
- Avrich, Paul. *An American Anarchist: The Life of Voltairine de* Cleyre. Princeton: Princeton University Press, 1978.
- ———. *The Haymarket Tragedy, The Modem School Movement: Anarchism and Education in the United States.* Princeton: Princeton University Press, 1980.
- ———. *Anarchist Portraits.* Princeton: Princeton University Press, 1988.
- ———. *Sacco and Vanzetti: The Anarchist Background.* Princeton: Princeton University Press, 1991.
- ———. *Anarchist Voices: An Oral History of Anarchism in America.* Princeton: Princeton University Press, 1995.
- ———. *The Modern School Movement: Anarchism and Education in the United States.* Princeton, N.J: Princeton University Press, 1980.
- Bailie, William. *Josiah Warren: The First American Anarchist.* Boston: Small, Maynard & Co., 1906.
- Baker, Keith Michael. "Closing the French Revolution: Saint-Simon and Comte." *The French Revolution and the Creation of Modern Political Culture*, Vol. 3. Eds. François Furet and Mona Ozouf. Oxford: Pergamon Press, 1989. 323-339.
- Barron, Hal S. *Those Who Stayed Behind: Rural Society in Nineteenth-Century New England.* Cambridge: Cambridge University Press, 1984.
- Becker, James F. *Marxian Political Economy: An Outline.* Cambridge: Cambridge University Press, 1977.
- Beecher, Jonathan. *Charles Fourier: The Visionary and his World.* Berkeley: California University Press, 1986.
- Berenson, Edward. "A New Religion of the Left: Christianity and Social Radicalism in France 1815--1848." *The French Revolution and the Creation of Modern Political Culture.* Vol. 3. Eds. François Furet and Mona Ozouf. Oxford: Pergamon Press, 1989. 543-560.
- Berry, Brian Joe Lobley. *America's Utopian Experiments: Communal Havens From Long-wave Crises.* Hanover: Dartmouth College, 1992.
- Berth, Édouard. "Proudhon En Sorbonne." *L'Independence* 27 (1912): 122-40.
- Berthod, Aimé. *Proudhon et la propriete. Un socialisme pour le paysan*, Paris: V. Giard & E. Brière, 1910.
- Berti, Giampietro D. *La Dimensione Libertaria Di Pierre-Joseph Proudhon.* Roma: Città Nuova, 1982.
- Bestor, Arthur E. Jr. "The Evolution of the Socialist Vocabulary." *Journal of the History of Ideas* 9, no. 3 (1948): 259-302.
- ———. *Records of the New Harmony Community.* Urbana: Illinois Historical Survey, 1950.
- ———. *Backwoods Utopias: The Sectarian Origins and Owenite Phases of Communitarian Socialism in America, 1663– 1829.* Philadelphia: University of Pennsylvania Press, 1971. 2nd edition.
- Blau Joseph, "Unfettered Freedom." *Transaction of the Charles S. Peirce Society* 7, no. 4 (1971): 243-258.

- Bodenhorn, Howard. *A History of Banking in Antebellum America: Financial Markets and Economic Development in an Era of Nation-Building*. Cambridge: Cambridge University Press, 2000.
- Bouglé, Celestin. *La Sociologie De Proudhon*. Paris: Armand Colin, 1911.
- Bourgeois, Nicolas, and Proudhon, Pierre Joseph. *Les théories du droit international chez Proudhon, le fédéralisme et la paix*. Paris: M. Rivière, 1927.
- Brogan, Denis William. *Proudhon*. London: Hamish Hamilton, 1934.
- Butler, Jon. "Magic, Astrology, and the Early American Religious Heritage, 1600-1760." The American Historical Review 84, no. 2 (1979): 317-346.
- Calhoun, Arthur W. *A Social History of the American Family from Colonial Times to the Present*. Vol. 2. Cleveland: The Arthur H. Clark Company, 1918.
- Carmony, Donald F., and Elliott, Josephine M. "New Harmony, Indiana: Robert Owen's Seedbed for Utopia." *Indiana Magazine of History* 76 (1980): 161-261.
- Carr, Edward Hallett. *Studies in Revolution*. London: Macmillan, 1950.
- Carter, April. *The Political Theory of Anarchism*. Routledge and K. Paul, London 1971.
- Chafuen, Alejandro Antonio. *Faith and Liberty: The Economic Thought of the Late Scholastics*. Lanham: Lexington Books, 2003.
- Chambost, Sophie. *Proudhon et la norme: Pensée Juridique d'un Anarchiste*. Rennes: Presses Universitaires de Rennes, 2004.
- Chase, Jeanne. "L'organisation de l'espace économique dans le nord-est des États-unis après la guerre d'independance." *Annales. Histoire, Sciences Sociales* 43, no. 4 (1988): 997-1020.
- Claeys, Gregory. "'Individualism,' 'Socialism,' and 'Social Science': Further Notes on a Process of Conceptual Formation, 1800-1850." *Journal of the History of Ideas* 47, no. 1. (1986): 81-93.
- ———. *Machinery, Money, and the Millennium: From Moral Economy to Socialism, 1815-1860*. Princeton, N.J.: Princeton Univ. Press, 1987.
- ———. *Citizens and Saints: Politics and Anti-Politics in Early British Socialism*. Cambridge: Cambridge University Press, 1989.
- *Owenite Socialism: Pamphlets and Correspondence*. London: Routledge, 2005.
- ———. "Non-Marxian Socialism 1815-1914." *The Cambridge History of Nineteenth-Century Political Thought*. Ed. Gareth Stedman Jones and Gregory Claeys. Cambridge: Cambridge University Press, 2011: 521-555.
- ———. "Early Socialism as Intellectual History." *History of European Ideas* 40, no. 7 (2014): 893--904.
- Clark, Barry. *Political Economy: A Comparative Approach*. New York: Preager, 1991.
- Clark, Christopher. *The Roots of Rural Capitalism: Western Massachusetts, 1780-1860*. Ithaca: Cornell University Press, 1990.
- Coclanis, Peter A. *The Shadow of a Dream: Economic Life and Death in the South Carolina Low Country, 1670-1920*. New York: Oxford University Press, 1989.
- Cohen, Daniel. *Not of the World, A History of the Commune in America*. Chicago: Follet Pub. Company, 1973.
- Cohen Henry, *Proudhon's Solution of the Social Problem*. New York: Vanguard Press, 1927.
- Cole, G. D. H. *A History of Socialist Thought: Vol. 1. Socialist Thought. The Forerunners 1789-1850*. London: Macmillan, 1953.
- Commons, John R., et al. eds. *A Documentary History of American Industrial Society*. Vol. 5. Cleveland, Ohio: The Arthur H. Clark Company, 1910.
- ———. *History of Labour in the United States*. New York: Macmillan, 1921.
- Conforti, Joseph. A. *Saints and Strangers: New England in British North America*. Baltimore: The Johns Hopkins University Press, 2005.
- Crowder, George. *Classical Anarchism: the Political Thought of Godwin, Proudhon, Bakunin, and Kropotkin*. New York: Oxford University Press, 1991.
- Cuvillier, Armand. *Proudhon*. Paris: Editions Sociales Internationales, 1937.
- Dana, Charles Anderson. *Proudhon and his "Bank of the People"*. New York: Benj. J. Tucker, 1896.

- Davis J. C. *Utopia and the Ideal Society: A Study of English Utopian Writing 1516-1700*. Cambridge: Cambridge University Press, 1981.
- ———. "The history of utopia: the chronology of nowhere." Utopias. Eds. Peter Alexander and Robert Gill. London: Duckworth, 1984. 1-18.
- ———. "Utopianism." The Cambridge History of Political Thought 1450-1700. Ed. J. H. Burns and Mark Goldie. Cambridge: Cambridge University Press, 1991. 329-44.
- DeLeon David. *The American as Anarchist: Reflections on Indigenous Radicalism*. Baltimore: Johns Hopkins University Press, 1978.
- Dolléans, Edouard. *Proudhon et la Révolution de 1848*. Paris: Presses Universitaires de France, 1948.
- Dorfman, Joseph. *The Economic Mind in American Civilization*. Vol. 1-3. New York: Viking Press, 1946-49.
- Douglas, Dorothy W. "P. J. Proudhon: A Prophet of 1848. Part I: Life and Works." *The American Journal of Sociology* 34, no. 5 (1929): 781-803.
- ———. "Part II. P.J. Proudhon: A Prophet of 1848." *The American Journal of Sociology* 35, no. 1 (1929): 35-59.
- Douty, H. M. "Word and the Deed-Anarchism Revisited, The [comments]." *Monthly Labor Review* 89, iss. 1 (1966): 15-18.
- Dupre, Daniel S. "The panic of 1819 and the political economy of sectionalism." *The Economy of Early America: Historical Perspectives & New Directions*. Ed. Cathy D. Matson. University Park, Pa: Pennsylvania State University Press, 2006: 263-293.
- Eckhardt, Cellia Morris. *Frances Wright: Rebel in America*. Cambridge: Harvard University Press, 1984.
- Ehrenberg, John. *Proudhon and his Age*. Atlantic Highlands, N.J.: Humanities Press, 1996.
- Elliott, Josephine. "The Owen Family Papers." *Indiana Magazine of History* 60, no. 4 (1964): 331--352.
- Ely, Richard T. *The Labor Movement in America*. New York: The Macmillan Company, 1905.
- Ernst, James Emanuel. *Ephrata: A History*. Allentown: Pennsylvania German Folklore Society, 1963.
- Fann, K. T. "Alexander Bryan Johnson (1786-1867): The First Linguistic Philosopher." *The Semiotic Web 1989*. Ed. Thomas A. Sebeok and Jean Umiker-Sebeok. Berlin, New York: De Gruyter, 1990.
- Feller, Daniel. *The Public Lands in Jacksonian Politics*. Madison: University of Wisconsin Press, 1984.
- Fellman, Michael. *The Unbounded Frame: Freedom And Community In Nineteenth Century American Utopianism*. Westport: Greenwood Press, 1973.
- Finkelstein, Barbara. *Governing the Young: Teacher Behavior in American Primary Schools, 1820--1880: a Documentary History*, New York: Columbia University Press, 1970.
- Fogarty, Robert S. *Dictionary of American Communal and Utopian History*. Westport, Conn.: Greenwood Press, 1980.
- Foner, Eric. "Radical Individualism in America: Revolution to the Civil War." *Literature of Liberty* 1, no. 3 (1978): 5-31.
- Forbes, Amy Wiese. "Let's Add the Stomach: Satire, Absurdity, and July Monarchy Politics in Proudhon's *What Is Property*?." *French Historical Studies* 24, no. 4 (2001): 679-705.
- Frayssé, Olivier. *Lincoln, Land, and Labor, 1809-60*. Urbana: University of Illinois Press, 1994.
- Frey, Donald E. "Individualist Economic Values and Self-Interest: the Problem in the Puritan Ethic." *Journal of Business Ethics* 17 (1998): 1573–1580.
- Gambone, Larry. *Proudhon's Libertarian Thought and the Anarchist Movement*. Montreal: Red Lion Press, 1996.
- George, William H. "Proudhon and Economic Federalism." *The Journal of Political Economy* 30 (1922): 531-542.
- Gilje, Paul. "The Rise of Capitalism in the Early Republic." *Journal of the Early Republic* 16, no. 2 (1996): 159-181.
- Gourevitch, Alex. *From Slavery to the Cooperative Commonwealth: Labor Republicanism and the Cooperative Commonwealth*. Cambridge: Cambridge University Press, 2015.

- Graham, H. "Political Theory and the Child: Problems of the Individualist Tradition." *Political Studies*, 27, no. 3 (1979): 405-420.
- Graham Robert, "The General Idea of Proudhon's Revolution.", http://dwardmac.pitzer.edu/Anarchist_Archives/proudhon/grahamproudhon.html (accessed 04.22.2015).
- Grinberg, Daniel. *Ruch anarchistyczny w Europie Zachodniej: 1870-1914*, Warszawa: PWN, 1994.
- Groenewegen, Peter. "Thomas Carlyle, "the Dismal Science" and the Contemporary Political Economy of Slavery", *History of Economics Review* 34 (2001): 74-94.
- Gray, John. *Mill on Liberty: A Defence*. London: Routledge, 1996.
- Guarneri, Carl. *The Utopian Alternative: Fourierism in Nineteenth-Century America*. Ithaca N.Y.: Cornell University Press, 1991.
- Guerin, D. "From Proudhon to Bakunin." *Our Generation* 17, no. 2 (1986): 23-33.
- Gurvitch, Georges. *Proudhon*. Paris: E. Dentu, 1965.
- Gutman, Amy, and D. Thompson, Dennis. *Democracy and Disagreement*. Cambridge: Harvard University Press, 1996.
- Halévy, Daniel. *Le Mariage de Proudhon*. Paris: Stock, 1955.
- Hall, Bowman N. "The Economic Ideas of Josiah Warren, First American Anarchist." *History of Political Economy*. 6.1 (1974): 95-108.
- ———. "The Economic Theories of Stephen Pearl Andrews: Neglected Utopian Writer." *South African Journal of Economics* 43, iss. 1 (1975): 28–34.
- ———. "Joshua K. Ingalls, American Individualist: Land Reformer, Opponent of Henry George and Advocate of Land Leasing, Now an Established Mode." *American Journal of Economics and Sociology* 39, no. 4 (1980): 383-396.
- Hall, Constance Margaret. *The Sociology of Pierre-Joseph Proudhon 1809-1865*. New York: Philosophical Library, 1971.
- Hampden, John. *Marx, Proudhon and European Socialism*. New York: Collier Books, 1966.
- Harbold, William H. "Justice in the Thought of Pierre-Joseph Proudhon." *Western Political Quarterly* 22 (1969): 723-741.
- Harrison, John F. C. *Robert Owen and the Owenites in Britain and America: Quest for the New Moral World*. New York: Charles Scribner's Sons, 1969.
- Haubtmann, Pierre. *La Philosophie Sociale De P.-J. Proudhon*. Grenoble: Presses Universitaires de Grenoble, 1980.
- ———. *Pierre-Joseph Proudhon: sa vie et sa pensée 1809-1849*. Paris: Desclée de Brouwer, 1982.
- Haulman, Clyde A. *Virginia and the Panic of 1819: The First Great Depression and the Commonwealth*. London: Pickering & Chatto, 2008.
- Hawley, Victor, and Fogarty, Robert S. *Special Love/special Sex: An Oneida Community Diary*. Syracuse, N.Y.: Syracuse University Press, 1994.
- Henretta, James. "Families and Farms: Mentalité in Pre-Industrial America," *The William and Mary Quarterly* 35, no. 1 (1987): 3-35.
- ———. *The Origins of American Capitalism: Collected Essays*. Boston: Northestern University Press, 1991.
- ———. "The 'market' in the Early Republic," *Journal of the Early Republic* 18, no. 2 (1998): 289--304.
- Hinds, William Alfred. *American Communities and Co-operative Colonies*. Chicago: Charles H. Kerr and Co., 1908.
- Hoffman, Robert. "Marx and Proudhon: A Reappraisal of Their Relationship." *The Historian* 29 (1967): 409-430.
- ———. *Revolutionary Justice: The Social and Political Theory of Pierre-Joseph Proudhon*. Urbana, IL: University of Illinois Press, 1972.
- ———. ed. *The Economy of Early America: The Revolutionary Period, 1763-1790*. Charlottesville: University Press of Virginia, 1988.
- Holloway, Mark. *Heavens on Earth: Utopian Communities in America, 1680-1880*. London: Turnstile Press, 1951.

■ Huston James L. "Virtue Besieged: Virtue, Equality, and the General Welfare in the Tariff Debates of the 1820s." *Journal of the Early Republic* 14, no. 4 (1994): 523-547.

■ ———. *Securing the Fruits of Labor: The American Concept of Wealth Distribution, 1765-1900.* Baton Rouge: Louisiana State University Press, 1998.

■ ———. "Economic Landscapes yet to Be Discovered: the Early American Republic and Historians' Unsubtle Adoption of Political Economy." *Journal of the Early Republic* 24, no. 2 (2004): 219--232.

■ Hyams, Edward. *Pierre-Joseph Proudhon.* London: John Murray (Publishers) Ltd; New York: Taplinger, 1979.

■ Innes, Stephen. *Creating the Commonwealth: The Economic Culture of Puritan New England.* New York: W.W. Norton, 1995.

■ Jacker, Corinne. *The Black Flag of Anarchy: Antistatism in the United States.* New York. Charles Scribner's Sons, 1968.

■ Jackson, J. Hampden. *Marx, Proudhon and European Socialism.* New York: Collier Books, 1962.

■ Jelenkowski, Marian. *Owen.* Warszawa: Wiedza Powszechna, 1981.

■ Jennings, Jeremy. *Revolution and the Republic: A History of Political Thought in France since the Eighteenth Century.* Oxford: Oxford University Press, 2013.

■ John, Richard R. *Spreading the News: The American Postal System from Franklin to Morse.* Cambridge, MA: Harvard University Press, 1995.

■ Johnson, Paul E. "The market revolution." *Encyclopedia of American Social History.* Vol. 1. Eds. Mary K. Cayton, Elliot J. Gorn, & Peter W. Williams. New York: Scribner, 1993. 545-560.

■ Jun, Nathan. "Review of *The Practical Anarchist: Writing of Josiah Warren,* by Crispin Sartwell," *Anarchist Studies* 20, no. 1 (2012).

■ Kanter, Rosabeth Moss. *Commitment and Community: Communes and Utopias in Sociological Perspective.* Cambridge, MA: Harvard University Press, 1972: 115-116.

■ Kauder, Emil. *A History of Marginal Utility Theory.* Princeton, NJ: Princeton University Press, 1965.

■ Kavenagh, W. Keith. *Foundations of Colonial America: A Documentary History.* Vol. 1. New York: Chelsea House, 1973.

■ Kelley, Donald R. *Historians and the Law in Postrevolutionary France.* Princeton. N.J.: Princeton University Press, 1984.

■ Kennedy, Roger G. *Mr. Jefferson's Lost Cause: Land, Farmers, Slavery, and the Louisiana Purchase.* New York: Oxford University Press, 2003.

■ Kesten, Seymour R. *Utopian Episodes: Daily Life in Experimental Colonies Dedicated to Changing the World.* Syracuse, N.Y.: Syracuse University Press, 1993.

■ Kimball, Janet. *The Economic Doctrines of John Gray 1799-1883.* Washington: Catholic Univ. of America Press, 1948.

■ King, John Edward. "Utopian or scientific? A reconsideration of the Ricardian socialists." *History of Political Economy* 15 (1983): 345-373.

■ Klein, Walter Conrad. *Johann Conrad Beissel: Mystic and Martinet, 1690-1768.* Philadelphia: University of Pennsylvania Press, 1942.

■ Knapp, Jeffrey. *An Empire Nowhere: England, America, and Literature from Utopia to the Tempest.* Berkeley: University of California Press, 1994.

■ Kolmerten, Carol A. *Women in Utopia: The Ideology of Gender in the American Owenite Communities.* Syracuse, N.Y.: Syracuse University Press, 1998.

■ Konig David Thomas. *Law and Society in Puritan Massachusetts: Essex County, 1629-1692.* Chapel Hill: University of North Carolina Press, 1979.

■ Kulikoff, Allan. "The Transition to Capitalism in Rural America." *William and Mary Quarterly* 46 (Jan. 1989): 120-44.

■ ———. *The Agrarian Origins of American Capitalism.* Charlottesville: University Press of Virginia, 1992.

■ ———. "The American Revolution, Capitalism, and the Formation of the Yeoman Classes." *Beyond the American Revolution: Explorations in the History of American Radicalism.* Ed. Alfred F. Young. DeKalb, Ill.: Northern Illinois University Press, 1993. 80-122.

■ Lakoff, Sanford A. "Socialism." *Dictionary of the History of Ideas, Studies of Selected Pivotal Ideas.* Vol. 4. Ed. Philip P. Wiener. New York: Charles Scribner's Sons, 1974: 284-294.

■ Larson, John Lauritz. *The Market Revolution in America: Liberty, Ambition, and the Eclipse of the Common Good.* Cambridge: Cambridge University Press, 2010.

■ Lawson, Donna. *Brothers and Sisters All Over This Land: America's First Communes.* New York: Praeger Publishers, 1972.

■ Lehning, Arthur. "Anachism." *Dictionary of the History of Ideas, Studies of Selected Pivotal Ideas.* Vol. 1. Ed. Philip P. Wiener. New York: Charles Scribner's Sons, 1974: 70-76.

■ Leopold, David. "Socialism and Utopia." *Journal of Political Ideologies* 12 (2007): 219-237.

■ ———. "Education and Utopia: Robert Owen and Charles Fourier." *Oxford Review of Education* 37 (2011): 619-635.

■ Leopold, Richard W. *Robert Dale Owen: A Biography.* Cambridge: Harvard University Press, 1940.

■ Leroy, Maxime. *Histoire des idées sociales en France.* Vol. 2. Paris: Gallimard, 1847.

■ Lockwood, George B. *The New Harmony Communities.* Marion, IN: The Chronicle Company, 1902.

■ ———. *The New Harmony Movement.* New York: D. Appleton and Co, 1905.

■ Longa, Ernesto A. *Anarchist Periodicals in English Published in the United States (1833-1955): An Annotated Guide.* Lanham, Md: Scarecrow Press, 2010.

■ Lubac, Henri de. *The Un-Marxian Socialist: A Study of Proudhon.* London: Sheed & Ward, 1948.

■ Lukes, Steven. "The Meanings of "Individualism"." *Journal of the History of Ideas* 32, no. 1 (1971): 45-66.

■ ———. "Individualism." *Dictionary of the History of Ideas, Studies of Selected Pivotal Ideas.* Vol. 2. Ed. Philip P. Wiener. New York: Charles Scribner's Sons, 1973-74. 595-604.

■ Martin, James Joseph. "American Prophets. I: Josiah Warren." *Liberation* 2 (1957): 10–14.

■ ———. *Men Against the State: The Expositors of American Individualist Anarchism, 1827-1908.* Colorado Springs: Ralph Myles, 1970.

■ Matson, Cathy D., ed. *The Economy of Early America: Historical Perspectives & New Directions.* University Park, PA: Pennsylvania State University Press, 2006.

■ McCoy, Drew R. *The Elusive Republic: Political Economy in Jeffersonian America.* Chapel Hill: University of North Carolina Press, 1980.

■ Merrill, Michael. "'Cash is Good to Eat': Self-Sufficiency and Exchange in the Rural Economy of the United States." *Radical History Review* 4 (1977): 42-71.

■ ———. "The Anticapitalist Origins of the United States," *Review (Fernand Braudel Center).* 13, no. 4 (1990): 465-497.

■ Mill, John Stuart. "Autobiography." *Collected Works of John Stuart Mill.* Vol. 1. Eds. John M. Robson and Jack Stillinger. Toronto: University of Toronto Press, 1981.

■ Miller, Perry. *The Marrow of Puritan Divinity.* Indianapolis: Bobbs-Merrill, 1937.

■ ———. *The New England Mind: From Colony to Province.* Cambridge: Harvard University Press, 1953.

■ Moment, Gairdner B., and Kraushaar Otto F. *Utopias, the American Experience.* Metuchen, N.J.: Scarecrow Press, 1980.

■ Moulin, Léo. "On the Evolution of the Meaning of the Word "Individualism"." *International Social Science Builletin* 7, no. 1 (1955): 181-185.

■ Muncy, Raymond Lee. *Sex and Marriage in Utopian Communities: 19th Century America.* Bloomington: Indiana University Press, 1973.

■ Mutch, Robert E. "Yeoman and merchant in pre-Industrial America: eighteenth-century Massachusetts as a case study." *Societas* 7 (1977): 279-302.

■ ———. "Colonial America and the Debate About Transition to Capitalism." *Theory and Society* 9 (1980): 847-863.

■ Nettlau, Max. "Anarchism in England fifty years ago. A contribution towards the elucidation of the science of society. By a member of the London Confederation of Rational Reformers." *Liberty, not the Daughter, but the Mother of Order* 15, no. 391 (1906): 44-45.

■ ————. "Anarchism: Communist or Individualist?—Both." *Mother Earth* 9, no. 5 (1914): 170-175.

■ ————. *Geschichte der Anarchie*, vol. 1-3 (Berlin: Asy-Verlag, 1925-1931).

■ Nicholson, Meredith. *The Hoosiers*. New York: MacMillan Company, 1926.

■ Noland, Aaron. "Proudhon and Rousseau." *Journal of the History of Ideas* 28 (1967): 33-54.

■ ————. "History and Humanity: The Proudhonian Vision." *The Uses of History: Essays in Intellectual and Social History*. Ed. Hayden White. Detroit: Wayne State University Press, 1968. 59-105.

■ ————. "Proudhon's Sociology of War." *The American Journal of Economics and Sociology* 29, no. 3 (1970): 289-304.

■ North, Douglass C. *The Economic Growth of the United States, 1790-1860*. Englewood Cliffs, N.J.: Prentice-Hall, 1961.

■ Noyes, John Humphrey. *A History of American Socialisms*. Philadelphia: J.B. Lippincott & Co, 1870.

■ Nozick, Robert. *Anarchy, State, and Utopia*. New York: Basic Books, 1974.

■ Oliver, W.H. "Owen in 1817: the Millenialist Moment." *Robert Owen: Prophet of the Poor*. Eds. Sidney Pollard and John Salt. London: Bucknell University Press, 1971. 166-188.

■ Osterud, Nancy Grey. "Gender and the Transition to Capitalism in Rural America." *Agricultural History* 67 (1993): 14-29.

■ ————. "Gender and the Capitalist Transition in Rural America." *History Teacher* 27 (1994): 273-276.

■ Oved, Yaacov. *Two Hundred Years of American Communes*. New Brunswick: Transaction Books, 1987.

■ Palmer, R. R. "Man and Citizen: Applications of Individualism in the French Revolution." *Essays in Political Theory Presented to George H. Sabine*. Eds. Milton R. Konvitz and Arthur Edward Murphy. Ithaca: Cornell University Press, 1948: 130-153.

■ Parrington, Vernon Louis. *Main Currents in American Though*. New York: Harcourt, Brace and Co., 1927.

■ ————. *American Dreams: A Study of American Utopias*. Providence: Brown University, 1947.

■ Peterson, Anna L. *Seeds of the Kingdom: Utopian Communities in the Americas*. Oxford: Oxford University Press, 2005.

■ Pitzer, Donald, ed. *America's Communal Utopias*. Chapel Hill and London: The University of North Carolina Press, 1997.

■ Podmore Frank. *Robert Owen: A Biography*. Vol. I-II. London: Hutchinson & Co., 1906.

■ Polanyi, Karl. *The Great Transformation: The Political and Economic Origins of our Time*. Boston, Mass.: Beacon Press, 2010.

■ Preucel, Robert W., and Pendery, Steven. "Envisioning Utopia: Transcendentalist and Fourierist Landscapes at Brook Farm, West Roxbury, Massachusetts." Historical Archaeology 40, no. 1 (2006): 6-19.

■ Pruitt, Bettye Hobbs. "Self-Sufficiency and the Agricultural Economy." *William and Mary Quarterly* 41 (1984): 333-64.

■ Puech, J. L. *Le proudhonisme dans l'association internationale des travailleurs*. Paris: F. Alcan, 1907.

■ Rede, Thomas Leman. *The Road to the Stage; Or, the Performer"s Preceptor*. London: Joseph Smith, 1827.

■ Reichert, William O. "Toward a New Understanding of Anarchism." *The Western Political Quarterly* 20, no. 4 (1967): 856-865.

■ ————. *Partisans of Freedom: A Study in American Anarchism*, Bowling Green, OH: Bowling Green State University Popular Press, 1976.

■ ————. "Natural Right in the Political Philosophy of P.J. Proudhon." *Law and Anarchism*. Eds. Thom Holterman and Henc Van Maarseveen. Montreal: Black Rose Books, 1984: 122-156.

■ Riesman, Janet A. "Money, Credit, and Federalist Political Economy." *Beyond Confederation: Origins of the Constitution and American National Identity*. Ed. R. R. Beeman et al. Chapel Hill: University of North Carolina Press, 1987. 128-161.

- ———. "Republican Revisions: Political Economy in New York after the Panic of 1819." *New York and the Rise of American Capitalism*. Ed. William Pencak and Conrad Edick Wright. Albany, NY: New York Historical Society, 1989: 1-44.
- Ritter, Alan. *The Political Thought of Pierre-Joseph Proudhon*. Princeton, N.J.: Princeton University Press, 1969.
- ———. "Godwin, Proudhon and the Anarchist Justification of Punishment." *Political Theory* 3 (1975): 69-87.
- Robbins, Lionel R., and Medema, Steven G., and Samuels Warren J. *A History of Economic Thought: The LSE Lectures*. Princeton: Princeton University Press, 1998.
- Robertson, H. M., and Taylor, W. L. "Adam Smith's Approach to the Theory of Value." *The Economic Journal* 67, no. 266 (1957): 181-198.
- Rocker Rudolf, and Briggs Arthur E. *Pioneers of American Freedom: Origin of Liberal and Radical Thought in America*. Los Angeles: Rocker Publications Committee, 1949.
- Roemer, Kenneth M. *America As Utopia*. New York: Burt Franklin, 1981.
- Rolland, Patrice. "La Fédéralisme, Un Concept Social Global Chez Proudhon." *Revue du Droit Public* (1993): 1521-1546.
- Roover Raymond de. "The Concept of the Just Price: Theory and Economic Policy." *The Journal of Economic History* 18, no. 4 (1958): 418-434.
- Ross, Stephen J. "The Transformation of Republican Ideology." *Journal of the Early Republic* 10, no. 3 (1990): 323-330.
- Rothbard, Murray. *The Panic of 1819: Reactions and Policies*. New York: Columbia University Press, 1962.
- ———. *For a New Liberty*. New York: Macmillan, 1973.
- ———. "Robert Nozick and the Immaculate Conception of the State." *The Journal of Libertarian Studies* 1, no. 1 (1977): 45–57.
- ———. *For a New Liberty: Libertarian Manifesto*. New York: Macmillan, 1978.
- ———. *An Austrian Perspective on the History of Economic Thought*. Vol. 1. Auburn, Alabama: Ludwig von Mises Institute, 2006.
- Rothenberg, Winifred B. *From Market-Places to a Market Economy: The Transformation of Rural Massachusetts, 1750-1850*. Chicago: University of Chicago Press, 1992.
- Rubel, Maximilien. "Non-Market Socialism in the Nineteenth Century." *Non-Market Socialism in the Nineteenth and Twentieth Centuries*. Eds. Maximilien Rubel and John Crump. Basingstoke: Palgrave Macmillan UK, 1987. 10-34.
- Runkle, Gerald. *Anarchism, Old and New*. New York: Delacorte Press., 1972.
- Sandefur, Timothy. "Liberal Originalism: A Past for the Future." *Harvard Journal of Law and Public Policy* 27, no. 2 (2004): 489-542.
- Sanders, Mike, ed. *Women and Radicalism in the Nineteenth Century (Subcultures and Subversions: 1750-1850)*. Vol. 2. London: Routledge, 2001.
- Sanders, John T., and Narveson, Jan. *For and Against the State: New Philosophical Readings*. Lanham, Md: Rowman & Littlefield, 1996.
- Sargant, William Lucas. *Robert Owen and His Social Philosophy*. London: Smith and Elder, 1860.
- Sartwell, Crispin. *The Practical Anarchist: Writings of Josiah Warren*. New York: Fordham University Press, 2011.
- Schuster, Eunice M. *Native American Anarchism: A Study of Left-Wing American Individualism*. Northampton, Mass., 1932.
- Schwartzman, Jack. "Ingalls, Hanson, and Tucker: Nineteenth-Century American Anarchism." *American Journal of Economics and Sociology* 62, iss. 5 (2003): 315–342.
- Sellers, Charles. *The Market Revolution: Jacksonian America, 1815-1846*. New York: Oxford University Press, 1991.
- Sherman, Howard. *Radical Political Economy: Capitalism and Socialism from a Marxist-Humanist Perspective*. New York: Basic Books, 1972.
- Silver-Isenstadt, Jean L. *Shameless: The Visionary Life of Mary Gove Nichols*. Baltimore: Johns Hopkins University Press, 2002.